YOUNG MATHEMATICIANS
AT WORK

YOUNG MATHEMATICIANS
AT WORK

CONSTRUCTING FRACTIONS, DECIMALS, AND PERCENTS

CATHERINE TWOMEY FOSNOT
MAARTEN DOLK

HEINEMANN • Portsmouth, NH

Heinemann
A division of Reed Elsevier Inc.
361 Hanover Street
Portsmouth, NH 03801-3912
www.heinemann.com

Offices and agents throughout the world

Screen shots reprinted by permission of Microsoft Corporation.

"Pizza Patterns" is reprinted from *Mathematics in Context: Some of the Parts.* Copyright ©1997. Reprinted by permission of the Encyclopædia Britannica, Inc.

The photo of the tapestry "L'artithmetique" is used courtesy of the Musée national du Moyen Age, Paris, Thermas at hotel de Cluny.

This material is supported in part by the National Science Foundation under Grant No. 9550080 and Grant No. 9911841. Any opinions, findings, and conclusions or recommendations expressed in this material are those of the authors and do not necessarily reflect the views of the National Science Foundation.

Library of Congress Cataloging-in-Publication Data

Fosnot, Catherine Twomey.
    Young mathematicians at work : constructing fractions, decimals, and percents /
Catherine Twomey Fosnot, Maarten Dolk.
        p. cm.
    Includes bibliographical references and index.
    ISBN 0-325-00355-6 (alk. paper)
    1. Mathematics—Study and teaching (Elementary). I. Dolk, Maarten Ludovicus
Antonius Marie, 1952– . II. Title.

QA135.5 .F6318 2002
372.7—dc21

                                                                    2001016587

Editors: Victoria Merecki and Leigh Peake
Cover design: Darci Mehall/Aureo Design
Cover photograph: Herbert Seignoret
Text photographs: Roseville Video and Herbert Seignoret
Manufacturing: Louise Richardson

Printed in the United States of America on acid-free paper

05   04   RRD   4   5

To the teachers with whom we have worked
and from whom we have learned so much

CONTENTS

CHAPTER 2: THE LANDSCAPE OF LEARNING

CHAPTER 3: EQUIVALENCE ON THE HORIZON

CHAPTER 9: TEACHERS AS MATHEMATICIANS

ACKNOWLEDGMENTS

The two names on the cover of this book mean only that we are the ones who finally sat down at the keyboard. The ideas included here grew out of a collaboration between researchers at the Freudenthal Institute and the faculty and staff of Mathematics in the City, a professional development program sponsored by the City College of New York. Together, we worked, reflected, talked, and experimented.

First and foremost, we thank our colleague Willem Uittenbogaard, whose voice is evident on every page. He has been an integral force in developing the project, designing and structuring the activities we use, and participating in our classroom investigations. He left the Netherlands and spent two years living and working in New York City, coteaching the institutes and follow-up courses and supporting teachers in their classrooms as they reformed their practice. We all grew to love him and respect his knowledge of mathematics, his understanding of the Freudenthal Institute's work, and his sensitivity to the cultural differences that are part of New York City. The mini-lessons built around problem strings (see Chapter 7) are largely the result of the work he did with us. He worked tirelessly to make the program a success, and we are extremely grateful for his professionalism, his generosity, and his dedication.

Staff members Sherrin Hersch, Betina Zolkower, Emily Dann, and Judit Kerekes all made important contributions as they helped teach the courses and worked alongside teachers in their classrooms. Sherrin also served as coprincipal investigator of the project, registering some 450 teachers in a myriad of courses, dealing with the paperwork, and acting as our liaison with the schools. This was often thankless, time-consuming work, and we acknowledge the hours she gave to it with such calmness and sanity. We are especially grateful for Betina's energy and her intellect, for the way she encouraged us to avoid trivialized word problems, pushing us instead to make the contexts rich and challenging. She was the adviser for many of the research projects teachers conducted in their classrooms. We thank Emily for the depth of mathematical knowledge she contributed and for commuting from Rutgers so tirelessly, always lending a supportive ear to our teachers and helping them in any way she could. We thank Judit for the many hours she volunteered because she believed in the project.

The project's smooth operation we owe to Herbert Seignoret. Hired initially as a part-time graduate assistant, he soon began working full time, helping with budgets, payroll, data collection, and general office management. We all came to rely on him and his amazing ability to do twenty things at once—and well.

In the fall of 2000, Toni Cameron, one of our original participants, became our coprincipal investigator, coordinating and leading inservice courses. Because of her superb and tireless work, we doubled our enrollment. We are extremely grateful for her wonderful energy and her willingness to take over the teaching Cathy had to let go in order to complete this manuscript.

We are especially grateful to the teachers and children whose voices— and real names—fill these pages. Without them and the things they tried in the classroom, the book could never have been written.

Many other colleagues read portions of the manuscript and provided helpful comments. In the spring of 2000, Cathy spent her sabbatical at the Freudenthal Institute in order to work on this three-volume series. While there, she shared an office with Koeno Gravemeijer, who read and commented on various portions of the manuscript and challenged us with his writing on models. In many ways, he helped bring the book to a higher level. Other colleagues from the Netherlands also read and commented on various portions of the manuscript: Ed de Moor, Frans van Galen, Jean Marie Kraemer, Anne Coos Vuurmans, and Arthur Bakker. Conversations with them helped us formulate the way we describe number relations. In particular, we want to thank Marja van den Heuvel-Panhuizen, from the Freudenthal Institute, who helped us design our approach to assessment and whose work is described throughout Chapter 8.

Funding for the project came from the National Science Foundation and the Exxon Educational Foundation. We are extremely grateful for their support. In the summer of 1999, we began to work with the city of New Rochelle Public Schools. We are grateful for their support. Some of the transcripts in the book are from lessons taught by these teachers.

Last, we thank our editors at Heinemann, Leigh Peake, Victoria Merecki, and Alan Huisman, for their belief in the project and for their insight.

PREFACE

This book is the final volume in a series of three. The first volume, *Young Mathematicians at Work: Constructing Number Sense, Addition, and Subtraction*, focuses on the development of numeracy in young children between the ages of four and seven. The second volume focuses on multiplication and division, particularly with children between the ages of seven and ten. This volume continues where volume 2 leaves off, focusing on how children between the ages of ten and thirteen construct their knowledge of fractions, decimals, and percents.

The series is a culmination of a long and fruitful journey—a journey characterized by collaboration, experimentation, reflection, and growth. More than ten years ago we learned of each other's work with teachers in our respective countries—Cathy in the United States, Maarten in the Netherlands. Both of us cared deeply about helping mathematics teachers base their practice on how people learn mathematics, how they come to see the world through a mathematical lens—how they come to *mathematize* their many worlds. Both of us had done research on teachers' beliefs and their visions of practice and how these beliefs and visions affected their decisions, and we were attempting to develop inservice programs that would enable teachers to reform their practice.

Cathy had previously been involved with the SummerMath for Teachers program, at Mt. Holyoke College, coteaching the summer institutes and working alongside elementary teachers in their classrooms. She had also developed and directed the Center for Constructivist Teaching, a graduate preservice program at Connecticut State University. Whether she was teaching children mathematics or helping teachers learn to teach, the learning psychology known as constructivism was at the core of her work.

Maarten, a researcher and developer at the Freudenthal Institute, in the Netherlands, had been involved in the development of inservice materials and multimedia learning environments for teachers. He had also directed the PANAMA inservice project in the Netherlands and been involved in implementing the "realistic mathematics" curricula, for which the Freudenthal Institute is now so widely known. Whether he was thinking about teaching children mathematics or helping teachers learn to teach, the didactic now commonly known as realistic mathematics was at the core of his work.

The focus in the United States was on how to develop learners' strategies and the big ideas surrounding them. And this was important. But the sequence of activities in the curricula being developed, even when supposedly aligned with the reform, was often based on the *discipline* of mathematics. For example, fractions were taught by way of simple part-to-whole shading activities in the lower grades, then in the higher grades as ratios, as partitioning, and finally as operators. Learners' methods of developing ideas and strategies were usually discussed in relation to pedagogy (principles of learning and teacher behavior that supports learning), if at all. Constructivist-based professional development helped teachers see the big ideas their learners were struggling with, but little attention was paid to *didactics*—a scientific theory of instruction relating to developing, stretching, and supporting mathematical learning over time. (In fact, the word *didactic* often has a negative connotation in the United States, one associated with self-correcting materials and direct instruction, not with development.)

In Europe the term *didactics* has a very different meaning. The French, for example, speak of situational *didactique,* meaning problems or situations that will enable learners to grow mathematically. The Dutch structure problem contexts in order to challenge and support learners developmentally. They spend years researching the effect of a sequence of carefully crafted problems. So, too, in Japan. Together, educators mold and craft problems in ways that strengthen their power to develop mathematical thinking. Teachers try these problems and then discuss which ones worked, which ones didn't, how they might be changed, what should come next.

The didactic in the Netherlands was based primarily on the work of the renowned mathematician Hans Freudenthal. As early as the sixties, Freudenthal had argued that people learn mathematics by actively investigating realistic problems. He claimed that mathematics was actually an activity of "mathematizing" the world, of modeling, of schematizing, of structuring one's world mathematically. Working with Dutch educators for over twenty years prior to his death in 1990, he was instrumental in reforming Dutch mathematics teaching based on "realistic mathematics." Within this framework, researchers formulated "learning lines" by studying the development of mathematical ideas historically, as well as the developmental progression of children's strategies and ideas about various mathematical topics. Then they crafted a series of contexts they thought might support children's natural development, often molding problems to facilitate disequilibrium or bring insights to the fore. Finally they tested these problems with children, revised them as necessary, and prepared them as curricula. Little attention was given to pedagogy or to cognitive psychology. While children were understood to move at their own pace developmentally, the class was taught as a whole. There was little attempt to support individual investigation or inquiry or to look at the belief systems of teachers regarding learning.

The American and Dutch educators both held important pieces of the puzzle. The Americans were thinking deeply about learning: how learners needed to engage in cognitive reordering; the importance of disequilibrium, reflection, and discussion; and the importance of big ideas. Teachers were analyzing their beliefs about learning and about their pedagogy. Classrooms were taking on the flavor of active workshops. But the Americans didn't know how to support development over time, how to use context as a didactic. The Dutch did.

In the late eighties we began to collaborate seriously. Cathy brought groups of teachers from Connecticut to the Netherlands for one-week intensive workshops, organized by Maarten and his colleague Willem Uittenbogaard. Maarten and other colleagues from the Freudenthal Institute (Jan De Lange, Frans van Galen) came to Connecticut State University. In 1993, Cathy left Connecticut State University and took a position at the City College of the City University of New York. We began to design a large-scale inservice program that would involve five school districts in New York City over five years, a project known as Mathematics in the City. The project was funded by the National Science Foundation and the Exxon Educational Foundation and began in 1995.

During the next five years we worked with over 450 elementary teachers in New York City and developed several demonstration sites. Our inservice program began with a two-week intensive institute focused on teaching and learning. In this beginning institute, we attempted to deepen teachers' knowledge of the mathematics they teach and to help them see themselves as mathematicians willing to raise questions, puzzle, and mathematize. Staff members then joined these teachers in their classrooms for a year, coteaching with them as they attempted to reform the way they presented mathematics. At the same time, participants took a course focused on children's strategies, the big ideas they grapple with, and the models they develop as they attempt to mathematize their world.

Throughout the project, we interviewed teachers, analyzed children's work, and videotaped lessons; together we constructed what we came to call a "landscape of learning." Classroom teachers continued to receive support as they collaborated with colleagues, and several went on to do field research and adjunct teaching with the program.

While our inservice project was successful, this series is not about the program per se. Throughout our five-year collaboration, we formulated new beliefs about learning and teaching mathematics. We challenged each other to go beyond our beginnings—to take our strengths to the table but to stay open and learn from each other. Together with our staff and our teachers, we entered new frontiers. This series offers stories from our classrooms and describes the ways we approach teaching and the contexts we use to promote investigations and inquiry.

ABOUT THIS BOOK

This book is about how middle school teachers in grades 5 through 8 can investigate fractions, decimals, and percents with their students. It is based on our collaboration and describes our current beliefs about teaching and learning mathematics. The structure of the book is similar to the previous two volumes, but the examples and the landscape of learning described are specific to fractions, decimals, and percents.

Chapter 1 describes and illustrates our beliefs about what it means to do and learn mathematics. We discuss it as *mathematizing*, but we ground it in the progression of strategies, the development of big ideas, and the emergence of modeling because we hold a constructivist view of learning.

Chapter 2 explains what we mean by a "landscape of learning." For teachers to open up their teaching, they need to have a deep understanding of this landscape, of the strategies, big ideas, and models children construct, of the landmarks they pass as they journey toward numeracy. This chapter also contrasts "word problems" with true problematic situations that support and enhance investigation and inquiry. It integrates the use of context as a didactic (realistic mathematics) with the cognitive psychology of constructivism. In order to teach in a way that truly enables young learners to "mathematize" their many worlds, classrooms must become communities of discourse. Rather than function as a transmitter in front of the classroom, teachers must "lead from behind." Children need to be able to take risks and investigate, and they must be willing to analyze errors and inadequate strategies. They must be able to represent, communicate, defend, and support their strategies and solutions with mathematical arguments. To that end, Chapter 2 also provides strategies that will help teachers turn their classrooms into math workshops.

Chapter 3 begins a journey of exploring the cultural and historical development of fractions and decimals and their equivalents. It traces the development of these ideas in Egypt, Babylonia, China, Greece, India, Arabia, and Europe and then offers examples of how children develop similar ideas and strategies. Several investigations undertaken by children and teachers in our classrooms illustrate ways to engage and support children as they construct the important strategies and big ideas related to this topic.

Chapter 4 continues the journey. It focuses on developing big ideas and strategies related to the landscape of learning. Again, there are several transcripts of children's investigations and conversations, along with samples of their work.

It is impossible to talk about mathematizing without talking about modeling. Chapter 5 defines what we mean by modeling and gives examples of how learners construct models as they try to make sense of their world mathematically. It also describes the importance of context in developing children's ability to model and shows how teachers can use the double number line, ratio tables, and open arrays as bridges between *models of situations* and *models as tools for thinking*.

Chapters 6 and 7 focus primarily on computation. Here we discuss what it means to calculate using number sense and whether or not the algorithms should still be seen as the goal of computation instruction. Although we conclude that children must be allowed to construct their own strategies, we offer many minilessons that will help children develop a repertoire of strategies based on a deep understanding of number relations and operations. We argue for the construction of a sense of "number space" comprising friendly numbers, neighbors, properties, and operations. We present examples of teachers using strings of related problems involving double number lines and open arrays to develop this sense of "number space."

In Chapter 8 we address how one assesses mathematizing. We describe performance and portfolio assessment, but we show how they can be strengthened by making the "mathematizing" more visible and by using the landscape of learning as a tool. We argue that assessment should inform teaching. We also share how children in Mathematics in the City classrooms fared on standardized achievement tests.

Last, in Chapter 9, we focus on the teacher as a learner. How do we help teachers begin to see themselves as mathematicians, be willing to inquire, work at their mathematical edge, and appreciate puzzlement? We open a window into an inservice classroom and invite you to mathematize along with the teachers we describe.

Like all human beings, mathematicians find ways to make sense of their reality. They set up relationships, they quantify them, and they prove them to others. For teachers to engage children in this process, they must understand and appreciate the nature of mathematics. They must be willing to investigate and inquire—and to derive enjoyment from doing so. The book you hold is primarily about that—how teachers and children come to see their own lived worlds mathematically, their journeys as they pursue the hard work of constructing big ideas, strategies, and mathematical models in the collaborative community of the classroom.

YOUNG MATHEMATICIANS
AT WORK

1 | "MATHEMATICS" OR "MATHEMATIZING"?

The United States suffers from "innumeracy" in its general population, "math avoidance" among high school students, and 50 percent failure among college calculus students. Causes include starvation budgets in the schools, mental attrition by television, parents [and teachers] who don't like math. There's another, unrecognized cause of failure: misconception of the nature of mathematics. . . . It's the questions that drive mathematics. Solving problems and making up new ones is the essence of mathematical life. If mathematics is conceived apart from mathematical life, of course it seems—dead.

—*Reuben Hersh*

The mathematician's best work is art, a high perfect art, as daring as the most secret dreams of imagination, clear and limpid. Mathematical genius and artistic genius touch one another.

—*Gösta Mittag-Leffler*

It is a truism that the purpose of teaching is to help students learn. Yet in the past teaching and learning were most often seen as two separate, even polar, processes. Teaching was what teachers did. They were supposed to know their subject matter and be able to explain it well. Students were supposed to do the learning. They were expected to work hard, practice, and listen to understand. If they didn't learn, it was their fault; they had a learning disability, they needed remediation, they were preoccupied, or they were lazy. Even when we spoke of development, it was usually in connection with assessing learners to see whether they were developmentally ready for the teacher's instruction.

Interestingly, in some languages, learning and teaching are the same word. In Dutch, for example, the distinction between learning and teaching is made only by the preposition. The verb is the same. *Leren aan* means teaching; *leren van* means learning. When learning and teaching are so closely related, they will be integrated in learning/teaching frameworks: teaching will be seen as closely related to learning, not only in language and thought but also in action. If learning doesn't happen, there has been no teaching. The actions of learning and teaching are inseparable.

Of course, different teachers have different styles of helping children learn. But behind these styles are frameworks based on teachers' beliefs about the learning/teaching process. These frameworks, in turn, affect how teachers interact with children, what questions they ask, what ideas they pursue, and even what activities they design or select. Teachers make many important decisions—some of them in a split second in the nitty-gritty of the classroom. In making these decisions, some teachers are led by the structure of mathematics or the textbook, others by the development of the children.

LEARNING AND TEACHING IN THE CLASSROOM

Join us in Carol Mosesson's fourth/fifth-grade classroom, in New Rochelle, New York. She is telling her students about a dilemma that occurred in her class the previous year and how she wants to be sure it doesn't happen again.*

"Last year," Carol explains, "I took my students on field trips related to the projects we were working on. At one point, we went to several places in New York City to gather research. I got some parents to help me, and we scheduled four field trips in one day. Four students went to the Museum of Natural History, five went to the Museum of Modern Art, eight went with me to Ellis Island and the Statue of Liberty, and the five remaining students went to the Planetarium. The problem we ran into was that the school cafeteria staff had made seventeen submarine sandwiches for the kids for lunch. They gave three sandwiches to the four kids going to the Museum of Natural History. The five kids in the second group got four subs. The eight kids going to Ellis Island got seven subs, and that left three for the five kids going to the Planetarium." As she talks, she draws a picture (see Figure 1.1) on chart paper of the context she is developing. "Now we didn't eat together, obviously, because we were all in different parts of the city. The next day after talking about our trips, several of the kids complained that it hadn't been fair, that some kids got more to eat. What do you think about this? Were they right? Because if they were, I would really like to work out a fair system—one where I would know how many subs to give each group when we go on field trips this year."

Carol is introducing fair sharing—a rich, real context in which her students can generate and model for themselves mathematical ideas related to fractions. When children are given trivial word problems, they often just ask themselves what operation is called for; the context becomes irrelevant as they manipulate numbers, applying what they know. Truly problematic contexts engage children in a way that keeps them grounded. They attempt to model the situation mathematically, as a way to make sense of it. They notice patterns, raise conjectures, and then defend them to one another.

---

*Although this investigation was embellished and situated in the context of field trips by Carol Mosesson, the kernel of the activity—fair sharing of submarine sandwiches—comes from Mathematics in Context, Encyclopaedia Britannica Educational Corporation.

"Turn to the person you are sitting next to and talk for a few minutes about whether you think this situation was fair," Carol continues.

"It's fair," several children comment. "It's one less sandwich than kids each time. It's three subs for four kids, so when there are five kids, they gave them four. For eight kids, they gave them seven."

"Yeah, but it wasn't fair for the Planetarium group. They had five kids and they only got three subs." Jackie is adamant as she comes to their defense. "The Museum of Modern Art group had five kids, too, and they got four sandwiches!"

"But you could just cut them in different pieces, like fourths or fifths," John offers.

"But the pieces would be different sizes. It's not fair."

"What do you think about her argument, John? Did everyone get the same amount?" Carol inquires, interested in whether John thinks the pieces would be equivalent. He shakes his head, acknowledging that the pieces would not be the same size. Another student raises his hand. "Michael?"

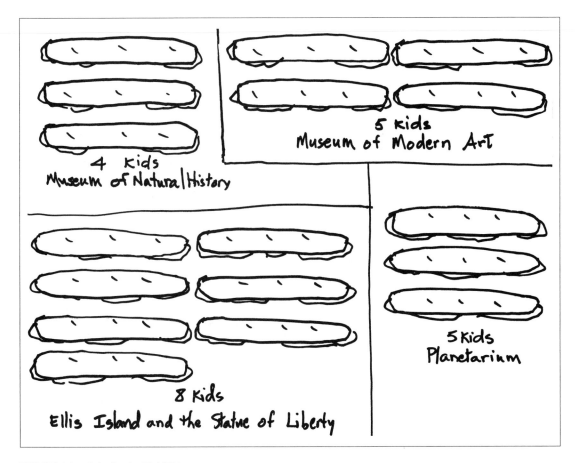

FIGURE 1.1   *Subs for the Field Trip*

"But the others *are* all the same." As Michael advances this common misconception, several of his classmates nod in agreement. "You keep adding one child and one sub. Three for four is the same as four for five."

"If the Planetarium group had another sub it would all be the same," Aysha says, verbalizing what most are thinking.

Carol has succeeded in making their initial ideas visible. Now she wants to create disequilibrium. "Well, let's investigate this some more. I suggest we work with our math workshop partners and check out two things." She writes the questions down on a large piece of chart paper as she talks. "How much did each child in each group get, assuming the subs were all shared equally in each group? And which group got the most?"

Several students continue to voice their agreement with Aysha and Michael. "I think they all got the same except for the Planetarium group."

"Well, let's check it out and see. Let's investigate a bit, prove your ideas, and we'll have a math congress after we've worked on it some. Use any materials you want, or make drawings to help you prove your thinking. We'll share our thinking when everyone feels he or she has had enough time to work on this."

The children set to work investigating the problem. Some take out Unifix cubes; most draw the subs and show how they would cut them. Carol moves from group to group, ensuring that everyone is busy and clear about the problem. She sits down with Jackie and Ernie for a moment.

"There were three subs for four kids," Jackie explains, "so we cut two subs in half, then the last in fourths. So everybody in that group got one half plus one fourth."

Ernie, her partner, explains their work for the Ellis Island group. "And we're doing the same thing here. See—we're giving each person a half sub first. That is four subs. One sub we're cutting into eight pieces, and the other two into fourths."

"So how much does each person in the group get?" Carol inquires.

"One half plus one eighth plus one fourth."

"And you're going to continue like this with the Planetarium and the Museum of Modern Art groups?" Jackie and Ernie nod yes. Carol notes their strategy: they are making unit fractions—fractions with numerators of one.

Nicole and Michelle, whom she visits next, have worked on the three-subs-four-kids situation very similarly. But for the four-subs-five-kids situation they have changed their strategy. Michelle explains, "We divided these subs up into fifths, because there were five kids."

Carol sees that each of the four subs is drawn and cut up into fifths. "So how much of a sub did each child get?" she asks.

"One of these, one of these, one of these, and one of these." Nicole points to a fifth from each sub. "That's four fifths of a sub for each kid because it is four times one fifth."

"Oh, that's interesting, isn't it? Four subs for five kids ended up being four fifths of a sub." Carol attempts to point up the relationship, but Nicole and Michelle seem uninterested, and they go back to using unit fractions for the seven-subs-eight-kids problem. Carol debates whether or not to suggest that they try the same strategy they used for the four-subs-five-kids situation but decides against it. They are very involved in the context and they (as well as Jackie and Ernie) are cutting up the subs in ways that make sense *within the context.* They can imagine subs cut up into halves, fourths, or even fifths. These are reasonable sizes. Eighths are not, unless they become necessary at the end to share a last sub fairly. The realistic nature of the context enables children to realize what they are doing, to check whether it makes sense.

Working within a context also develops children's ability to make mathematical meaning of their own many lived worlds. There is much to be investigated yet. Asking children to adopt multiplication and division shortcuts too soon may actually impede genuine learning. As the well-known mathematician George Polyá (1887–1985) once pointed out, "When introduced at the wrong time or place, good logic may be the worst enemy of good teaching." Historically (see the in-depth discussion in Chapter 3), unit fractions were used for a very long time before common fractions were accepted. As the children explore fair-sharing situations with unit fractions, they will have experiences comparing and making equivalent fractions. These experiences will bring up some big ideas and support the development of some powerful mathematical strategies. Let's return to Jackie and Ernie at work to witness this process.

Jackie has drawn four subs, and she and Ernie are deciding how to share this amount fairly among five kids—the ones who went to the Museum of Modern Art. "Let's give everyone a half again first. That leaves one and a half subs left."

"So let's cut the whole one up into fifths." Ernie draws four lines, making five equal parts, as he talks.

"Okay, so now every kid has one half plus one fifth," Jackie continues, "and now we have to cut up the last half into fifths. So it's one half plus one fifth plus—one fifth? That can't be—these are just slivers." She points to the small pieces resulting from cutting up the half sub. "These slivers are only about half the size of those fifths. So what do we call these?"

Jackie and Ernie are struggling with a big idea. To resolve their puzzlement they must grapple with the heart of fractional relationships. One fifth of a half sub is smaller than one fifth of a whole sub. What is the whole? And what is the equivalence of this piece to the whole?

"You're right—two of these fifths [the slivers] are about the same as one of those fifths," Ernie ponders. "So maybe it's a half of a fifth. But what is that?"

"We know it is a fifth of a half of a sub—"

"Yeah, but it is also one half of a fifth—see." Ernie points out the relationship of the sliver to the fifths that resulted when one sub was cut into five equal pieces. He is noticing that $\frac{1}{2} \times \frac{1}{5} = \frac{1}{5} \times \frac{1}{2}$. This relationship is a specific example of the commutative property of multiplication, although for him at this point it is probably not generalizable.

"Well, if it's a half of a fifth, then it must be a tenth," Jackie offers.

Ernie ponders her suggestion and then finds a way to prove it. "Oh, I get it—look. If this half is cut into fifths to make the slivers, then the other half could be too. And then—you're right—there's ten pieces in the whole sub. So one fifth of a half is one tenth."

"So now the Planetarium group is easy. Everybody gets a half plus one tenth!" Jackie draws the subs for the last scenario, showing the fair sharing (see Figure 1.2). "Now all we have to do is compare them!"

David Hilbert (1897), in his book, *Report on Number Theory,* wrote, "I have tried to avoid long numerical computations, thereby following Riemann's postulate that proofs should be given through ideas and not voluminous computations." As they set out to compare the four scenarios and prove which group got the most, Jackie and Ernie could add up the fractional parts

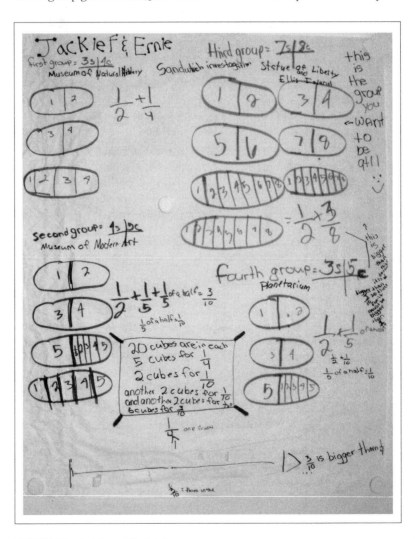

FIGURE 1.2 *Jackie and Ernie's Strategy*

and make common denominators, but they don't. Working with unit fractions has allowed them to hit upon a brilliant strategy to make the problem simpler.

"Everybody, in every group, got a half. So we can eliminate that," Jackie suggests.

"So all we have to do is compare the remainders," Ernie finishes her thought. "So we have one fourth for the Museum of Natural History group, one fifth plus one tenth for the Museum of Modern Art group, one fourth plus one eighth for the Ellis Island group, and one tenth for the Planetarium group.

"The Ellis Island group got one eighth more than the Museum of Natural History group."

"And the Museum of Modern Art group got one fifth more than the Planetarium group."

"But how do we compare the others?"

Ernie grabs some Unifix cubes, "I have an idea! What's a good number to use?" He ponders for a moment then clarifies for Jackie, "I'm trying to think of a number that we could use to build the subs—a number that five and four and ten would go into—"

"How about twenty?" Jackie offers.

"Yeah—that's good." Ernie counts out twenty cubes and builds a stack with them to represent a sub. "Okay—so the fourth is five cubes, the fifth is the same as two tenths . . . and one tenth more, that's three tenths." As they begin to combine amounts and use twenty as a common denominator, they make a first attempt at generating common fractions. Jackie continues, "Ten times two is twenty, so two, four, six—three tenths is the same as six twentieths. That's more than five twentieths!"

At first the eighths stump them: eight does not go into twenty evenly. But Ernie returns to their drawing. Using his fingers, he points to each eighth and says, "Two of these make a fourth—so the Ellis Island group got three eighths."

Jackie excitedly finishes the comparison. "Eighths are bigger than tenths. We're comparing three eighths to three tenths. If you cut up a sub into tenths, those pieces are smaller than if you cut it up into eighths. The threes are the same on the top," referring to the numerators, "so the Ellis Island group got the most—three eighths of a sub!"

"Plus the half," Ernie reminds her. "And the Planetarium group got the least. One tenth is the littlest because if you divide a sub into fourths or fifths or tenths—the more pieces you have the smaller the piece is! They only got a half plus one tenth!"

What Is Revealed

This glimpse into Carol's classroom reveals a very different approach to mathematics from the one most of us experienced in our past schooling. Traditionally mathematics has been perceived as a ready-made discipline to be handed down by a teacher skilled in the art of transmitting, or explaining, clearly. In the classrooms most of us have attended, teachers stood at the chalkboard and explained fractions as shaded parts of a whole. They taught rules for making common denominators. They demonstrated procedures for operations with fractions, like invert and multiply, and students practiced them over and over. Some teachers may have used fraction bars or pattern blocks to demonstrate, hoping to develop understanding. But the premise was always the same. The teacher was the fountain of wisdom who understood that mathematics was a discipline thought to comprise facts, concepts, formulas, and algorithms, and this discipline could be transmitted, explained, practiced, and learned if teachers were well versed in it and learners were diligent. Most students in mathematics classrooms did not see mathematics as creative but instead as something to be explained by their teacher, then practiced and applied. One might call this traditional approach "school mathematics."

Mathematicians, on the other hand, engage in quite a different practice. They make meaning in their world by setting up quantifiable and spatial relationships, by noticing patterns and transformations, by proving them as generalizations, and by searching for elegant solutions. They construct new mathematics to solve real problems or to explain or prove interesting patterns, relationships, or puzzles in mathematics itself. The renowned mathematician David Hilbert once commented that he liked to prove things in at least three or four different ways, because by doing so he better understood the relationships involved. At the heart of mathematics is the process of setting up relationships and trying to prove these relationships mathematically in order to communicate them to others. Creativity is at the core of what mathematicians do.

Interestingly, the sculptor Henry Moore described his work in much the same way Hilbert did. He said that before he sculpted something, he always drew the figure several times to learn more about it. In fact, we all find ways to make meaning from our interactions in the world. The process of constructing meaning *is* the process of learning. We create our knowledge; we do not discover it. Writers make meaning when they formulate stories and narratives, when they construct characters and plots, when they play with words and metaphors. Scientists make meaning by wondering about scientific phenomena; by hypothesizing, designing, and performing experiments; and then by proposing explanations that fit their results. Musicians hear cadence, rhythm, harmony, discordance, and melody as they interact in their world. Artists see color, form, texture, and line.

In fields other than mathematics, we've understood this constructive nature of learning. We teach students to become good writers by involving them in the process of writing. In science, we engage learners in actively inquiring, in formulating hypotheses, and in designing experiments. We teach art by allowing learners to create their own "masterpieces." Have we traditionally been teaching mathematics in our classrooms or only the "history" of mathematics—some past mathematicians' constructions and their applications? Is there any connection at all between "school mathematics" and "real mathematics"?

The vignette from Carol's classroom is evidence of a different view of mathematics—one more closely akin to the process of constructing meaning, one that might better be termed *mathematizing*. Children are finding ways to explore situations mathematically, they are noticing and exploring relationships, putting forth explanations and conjectures, and trying to convince one another of their thinking—all processes that beg a verb form. This view of mathematics was put forth by the well-known twentieth-century Dutch mathematician Hans Freudenthal (1968) when he argued that mathematics was a human activity—the process of modeling reality with the use of mathematical tools.

To generate such mathematizing, Carol immerses her students in an investigation grounded in context. As they examine the fair-sharing situation and develop their own strategies for dealing with it, they find ways to simplify the numbers by pulling them apart. They notice relationships. Then they explore these relationships and try to figure out why they are happening. They raise their own mathematical questions and discuss them in the mathematical community of their classroom. But is this only process? What about content? Do all the children construct an understanding of fractions? Is this the goal that day for all the children? What does it mean to "understand" fractions?

Back to the Classroom

Let's return to Carol's classroom as she continues to visit with and question her students. Three children, Michael, Gabrielle, and Ashleigh, are sitting on the floor with big chart paper in front of them, on which they have drawn big subs. Carol joins them. "So tell me what you're doing. How are you guys thinking about this?"

"Our drawing shows how we cut up the subs," reports Ashleigh. "It wasn't fair. The cafeteria staff did make a mistake. Now we're trying to figure out which group got more."

Teachers often confuse right answers with understanding. Right answers are of course important, but they are not sufficient. Carol probes further, "And how are you thinking about that?" she asks.

Michael explains, "We were thinking that if we gave everybody half a sub, then we could tell." At first Carol thinks their strategy is the same as Jackie and Ernie's, but as Michael continues she realizes that they are not completing the division—they are not thinking relationally. "When we get rid of the halves, the Ellis Island group has three subs left, the Museum of Natural History group has one left, the Museum of Modern Art group has one and a half subs left, and the Planetarium group has only half a sub left. Three is the most!"

Carol realizes that although their answer is correct—the Ellis Island group did get the most—their thinking is not. "But how do you know that three subs is more—don't the remainders get shared too? Don't the three subs have to be shared with the eight kids? The one-and-a-half subs only have to be shared with five kids, and here," she points to the three-subs-four-kids scenario, "you have one sub left to share with four kids. Eight is more people, so how do you know which is more?" Michael looks puzzled as he realizes Carol's point.

Gabrielle comes to his rescue, but her thinking is not solid either. "One sub for four people, that's one fourth, and here," she points to the one-and-a-half-sub remainder, "one sub for five people is one fifth. One fifth is more than one fourth." This misconception is common when children begin to explore fractions. The whole number five is more than four, so why wouldn't one fifth be more than one fourth? One of the benefits of exploring fractions using a fair-sharing situation is that this misconception is easily dispelled.

Ashleigh disagrees, "No, one fourth is more than one fifth."

Now Gabrielle looks puzzled. "No." She shakes her head, continuing to ponder the subs being cut. Then, realizing that Ashleigh is right, she slowly agrees. "Oh—yeah."

"Convince me," Carol challenges Gabrielle.

"When you share with five people the pieces are smaller than with four." Gabrielle is clear.

Carol continues probing, "What about this half sub remaining in the Planetarium group? It still has to be shared with five people. How much will they get? Is that one fifth too?"

All three children are at first quiet as they puzzle over Carol's question, but Ashleigh thinks it through, "No, it is one fifth of half a sub. That's one tenth."

"Can you prove that to us, Ashleigh?" Carol continues to push for mathematical thinking—to go beyond just answers.

"If you cut the other half into five pieces too, the sub is cut into ten pieces. So each of the fifths of one half is one tenth of the whole thing." She points to the pieces as she talks, and Gabrielle and Michael are convinced by her explanation. Carol concurs and then suggests that they continue exploring which group got more. She moves on to Jennifer and John.

These two children have modeled the problem like Nicole and Michelle did in the four-subs-five-kids situation, but they have done so consistently (see Figure 1.3). Jennifer explains, "We cut up every sub into the number of people. See. Three subs for four people was three fourths, and four subs for five people was four fifths."

Carol asks, "Show me how you got three fourths for each child."

"It's just one fourth out of each sub, and there's three subs."

"And this worked every time?" Carol pushes for generalization. "Wow, what a great shortcut! Can you come to math congress being able to prove that this procedure would always work—that the number of subs divided by the number of people is how much of each sub everyone will get?" They nod enthusiastically, pleased with their solution, and they set out to find a way to prove it to their classmates.

As she moves from group to group, Carol's questioning changes in relation to what the children are investigating and the ideas and strategies each child is in the process of constructing. Although the connection between fractions and division is an overall "horizon"—an overall goal purposely embedded in the context—each child is at a different place developmentally, and therefore the context is open enough to allow for individual exploration and divergence.

Carol continues to support and encourage development as she leads the subsequent *math congress.* In a math congress, the whole class gathers and children present and discuss their strategies and solutions with one another.

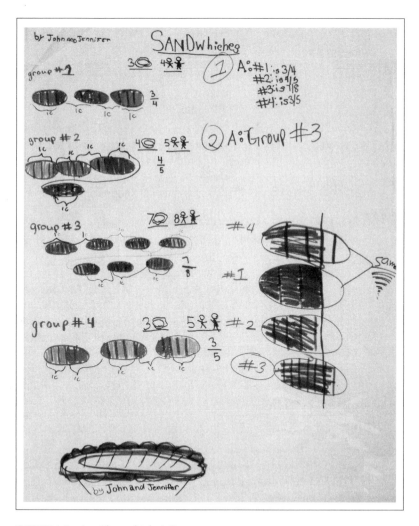

FIGURE 1.3   *Jennifer and John's Strategy*

Just as mathematicians work out formal proofs to convince their fellow mathematicians of the relationships they have been exploring, Carol's students defend and support their thinking as Carol guides their discussion to develop important mathematical ideas and strategies. The math congress is much more than just sharing; it is a critical part of the math lesson. As children prepare to present their work, and as they think about how they will communicate their work and anticipate their classmates' questions, their own understanding deepens.

As Carol plans for the math congress, she thinks about how she will structure it, which group she will start with, on which ideas she will focus, how she will make sure that everyone is challenged. Not everyone will share. There is not enough time, nor is that the goal. Carol will use the congress to focus on a few critical ideas. Should she just have a group share that can explain their thinking well? A group with an elegant solution? A group she didn't get to, so that she can see what they did? Would any of these pedagogical strategies support development? How *will* she continue to support development?

The Math Congress

"Gabrielle, Michael, and Ashleigh, please start us off." Carol decides to have this group share. Their solution is similar to most: it will prompt a good discussion of equivalence. But she also chooses to have this group share, rather than Jackie and Ernie, *because they have struggled.* Carol hopes that the process of *explaining their thinking* to their classmates will develop even further clarity for them.

The group members come to the front of the class with their chart (see Figure 1.4) and post it on the chalkboard with small magnets. Ashleigh begins. "We gave everybody a half first. In the Planetarium group—three subs, five kids—we were left with half a sub. We had to share that, too, so we cut that up into five pieces. Each of those was one fifth of one half. That was one tenth. So in this group everyone got one half plus one tenth."

Ashleigh has been confident and clear. Carol looks around and sees that everyone appears to agree. To check she asks, "How many of you can put in your own words where they got the one tenth?" Many hands are up, since this was an idea that many of the children had grappled with as they worked. Carol asks Christina, a child she did not get to as she moved around the room, to paraphrase, and Christina is able to do so clearly.

Gabrielle continues with the next situation—three subs, four kids. "We did the same thing here. We were left with one sub, which we cut into four pieces. Everyone in this group got one half plus one fourth, or three fourths."

Michael, explaining the equivalence, adds, "Right. See—two of these fourths make one half, so one fourth more is three fourths." Once again their classmates nod agreement. When the group moves on to the Museum of Modern Art situation—four subs, five kids—however, a spirited discussion ensues.

"Everybody in this group got four fifths of a sub. We cut each sub up into fifths, and each person got four times one fifth," Ashleigh explains. As they were preparing for the congress, they redrew this scenario. Their drawing looks very different to Ernie, who has also used an "elimination of halves" strategy. He thought he was following the discussion. Now he is puzzled. "I don't understand," he blurts out. "You just have numbers floating all over your drawing. What do they represent?"

Christina also is confused. "I don't get it either," she declares, "if each person gets one fifth of each sub, isn't there four fifths left over?"

"You gave them each five pieces," another student argues provocatively. "There's two ones in the first sub, and then three more ones. That's five pieces!"

Carol realizes that the numbers on the chart refer to the pieces, not the children. They are counting the pieces each child gets, not distributing pieces

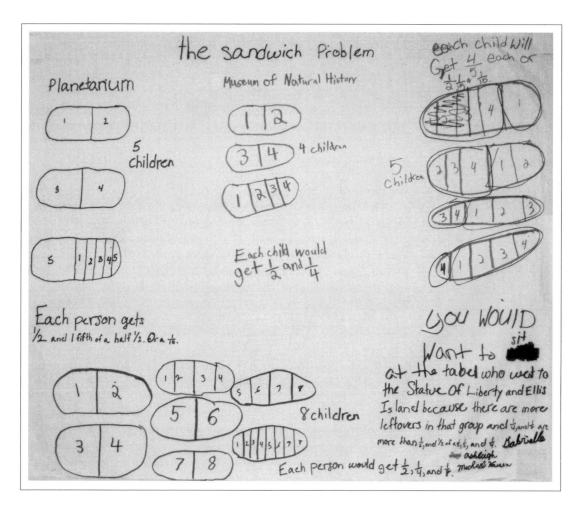

FIGURE 1.4   *Gabrielle, Michael, and Ashleigh's Strategy*

to children. As they drew the picture to get ready for the congress, it took on a different meaning. It represents the result of an action that for them is now almost mental. It represents their answer rather than the process of the distribution. To help clarify this Carol asks, "Where is the fifth child in your drawing? Why don't you use a marker and circle the children for us."

Ashleigh circles groups of four fifths, and it now becomes apparent to her classmates what the numerals in the drawing represent.

"Oh, I get it!"

"Oh, yeah."

"But how did you know it would be four fifths?" Ernie wonders.

Michael explains how they went from eliminating the halves to the representation they are now discussing. "We started with a half and we were left with one-and-a-half subs that we still had to share with five people. We cut up the whole into fifths, and then the one half into fifths. But those pieces were really tenths—because they were fifths of one half." His classmates appear to be following his thinking, so he continues. "The one half is between the two and the three." He points to the picture. "One half is equal to two-and-one-half fifths. It's in the middle. Another tenth makes it three fifths, and then plus the last one fifth. So it is four fifths." A few students still look puzzled; others are intrigued and amazed.

Ashleigh continues to clarify, shading in the one half with the marker she still holds, answering her own question. "Where is the half?"

"Oh, in between!"

"Two-and-one-half fifths!"

"Oh, I get it!

"And the one tenth makes it three fifths."

Their thinking awes Christina. "And so how did you decide which group got the most?"

"We thought it was between the Ellis Island group, which got one fourth plus one eighth plus the half, and the Museum of Modern Art group, which got one tenth plus one fifth plus the half," Michael explains. "We knew the halves could be removed, so we just compared the rest. One fourth is more than one fifth, and one eighth is more than one tenth—because you are dividing by more people. The more pieces you cut, the smaller they have to be to fit in the whole sandwich."

Michael, Ashleigh, and Gabrielle have made a huge jump in thinking as they have worked through this investigation. Starting with eliminating halves and comparing remainders as whole numbers (not in relation to the number of children), they progressed to unit fractions. As they attempted to represent their thinking, they combined the unit fractions into common fractions. They are now solid on understanding that the bigger the denominator, the smaller the fraction. The thinking apparent as they communicate and prove their strategy to their fellow classmates is remarkably different from their thinking an hour before.

Carol has successfully used the math congress to support these students' growth. But she has also used this discussion to bridge the unit fraction strategy with the use of common fractions for the class as a whole. As she continues with the congress, the scaffolds she provides—the way in which she supports development—become even more apparent. "John and Jennifer, your strategy was quite different. Would you share next?"

John and Jennifer describe how they cut each sub into a number of parts that matched the number of people. They show how each piece times the number of subs results in how much each person gets.

Jackie notices the relationship before they can finish. "Hey! Their answers are the same as the numbers in the problem. It's just the number of sandwiches divided by the number of people!"

"Oh, wow!"

"So weird!"

"Will that always work? Why is that happening?" Carol pushes for generalization. "It's just division!" Jackie exclaims. "Twelve subs shared by four people is twelve divided by four equals three. Four subs shared with twelve people is four divided by twelve. It's one twelfth, four times!"

What Is Revealed

By varying her questioning as she monitors the congress, Carol allows her students to think further about their strategies and gives them a chance to "stretch" mathematically from wherever they are developmentally. By constructing their own strategies and defending them, all the children are immersed in an investigation that involves mathematizing. But mathematizing should not be dismissed simply as process. Mathematizing *is* content. Children are exploring ideas—fair sharing, equivalence, and common denominators; the connection between fractions, division, and multiplication; common fractions—in relation to their own level of cognitive development. As children learn to recognize, be intrigued by, and explore patterns, and as they begin to overlay and interpret experiences, contexts, and phenomena with mathematical questions, tools, and models (such as the fair-sharing one in this problem), they are constructing what it really means to be a mathematician. They are learning to organize and interpret their world through a mathematical lens. This is the essence of mathematics.

Carol supports her students by posing questions and offering rich contexts for mathematizing. This approach enables children to take the next step in the learning process. The development of the children seems to guide Carol's teaching. But development can be nothing more than a catchword. No one would disagree that development is important. Educators have talked about developmentally appropriate practice for years. But what does development mean *in relation to mathematics learning and teaching?*

Carol's teaching reflects her appropriate understanding of development. But she does more—she employs a different framework. Her teaching is grounded in the development of *mathematical ideas*—in her knowledge of the structure of mathematics. But there is still more. She understands the paths and the horizons of the landscape of this learning; she knows how children *come to understand* different mathematical ideas. She thinks about how to employ mathematical contexts as a didactic—how to use them to facilitate mathematical learning. She knows and recognizes important landmarks along the way—strategies, big ideas, and mathematical models—and she designs her contexts with these landmarks in mind. Different contexts have the potential to generate different models, strategies, and big ideas. In Carol's framework, learning and teaching are connected. She works on the edge between the structure of mathematics and the development of the children; the value she gives one or the other differs with what happens in her classroom.

STRATEGIES, BIG IDEAS, AND MODELS IN A TEACHING/LEARNING FRAMEWORK

Strategies as Schemes

The mind is never a blank slate. Even at birth, infants have organized patterns of behavior—or schemes (Piaget 1977)—for learning and understanding the world. Beginning as reflexes (grasping and orienting, for example), these initial schemes soon become differentiated and coordinated. Children learn to crawl and then walk to objects to be grasped, felt, sucked, and explored visually. Grasping is refined to include pushing, pulling, hitting, and other forms of exploring with the fingers. Sucking is differentiated into chewing, biting, and licking. New strategies for exploration are constructed.

Children attempting to understand "how many"—how many plums there are in the grocer's box, how many stairs they have climbed after going up ten flights, how many boxes are needed to hold 296 candies, how much of a submarine sandwich everyone got—use various assimilatory schemes. They count by ones or skip count by groups. They work with familiar pieces first (how many tens in one hundred, for example). They cut up the subs and share them and turn the ratio of subs to people into unit fractions—a *unit fractioning* strategy. These strategies in turn evolve into efficient *strategies for equivalence* (making common fractions) and *strategies for computation* (operations with fractions).

Developing all these strategies is no mean feat! The progression of strategies, or "progressive schematization" as Treffers (1987) calls it, is an important inherent characteristic of learning.

Big Ideas as Structures

Underlying this developmental progression of strategies is the construction of some essential big ideas. What is a "big idea" and how is it different from a strategy?

Big ideas are "the central, organizing ideas of mathematics—principles that define mathematical order" (Schifter and Fosnot 1993, 35). As such, they are deeply connected to the structures of mathematics. They are, however, also characteristic of shifts in learners' reasoning—shifts in perspective, in logic, in the mathematical relationships they set up. As such, they are connected to part/whole relationships—to the structure of thought in general (Piaget 1977). In fact, that is *why* they are connected to the structures of mathematics. As mathematical ideas developed through the centuries and across cultures, the advances were often characterized by paradigmatic shifts in reasoning. These ideas are "big" because they are critical to mathematics and because they are big leaps in the development of children's reasoning.

For example, *the greater the denominator, the smaller the fraction* is one big idea we saw children grappling with in Carol's class. Another was the idea that *the whole matters*—one fifth of one half is one tenth of a whole sub. Still another is that *fractions are connected to division and multiplication*—four fifths is four divided by five, or one divided by five four times. To construct these ideas, children have to grapple with new perspectives, new ways of interpreting relationships—realizing that fair sharing can be represented as unit fractions or as common fractions, for example. This is a huge shift in thinking for children and, in fact, was a huge shift in mathematics that took centuries to develop!

Models as Tools for Thought

Language was constructed to signify meaning. When we construct an idea, we want to communicate it: through time and across cultures humans have developed language as a way to do so. Initially, language represents ideas and actions; it is *a representation of thought.* Eventually it serves as *a tool for thought.*

Numerals were developed to signify the meaning of counting. Operational symbols like × and ÷ were constructed to represent the actions of combining and portioning equivalent-size groups. Ratio tables, rational numbers, decimals, and percents were developed as ways to signify relation. While these symbols were initially developed to represent mathematical ideas, they become tools, mental images, to think with.

To speak of mathematics as mathematizing demands that we address mathematical models and their development. To mathematize, one sees, organizes, and interprets the world through and with mathematical models. Like language, these models often begin simply as representations of situations, or problems, by learners. For example, learners may initially represent a situation with Unifix cubes, as Jackie and Ernie did when they represented the sub with twenty cubes, or with drawings that show the fair sharing and equivalent parts. These models of situations eventually become generalized as learners explore connections between and across them.

Teachers can use models as a didactic to transfer learning from informal solutions specific to a context to more formal, generalizable solutions—to bridge models *of* thinking with models *for* thinking (Beishuizen et al. 1997; Gravemeijer 1999). For example, using ratio tables or double number lines or

open arrays to represent children's computation strategies (see Chapters 5
and 7) can enable children to develop a sense of "number space"—a mental image of number based on relationships and operations (Lorenz 1997).

Walking the Edge

Carol walks the edge between the structure of mathematics and the development of the child by considering the progression of strategies, the big ideas
involved, and the emergent models. Ultimately what matters is the mathematical activity of the learner—how the learner mathematizes the situations
that Carol designs. But learning—development—is complex. Strategies, big
ideas, and models are all involved—they all need to be developed as they
affect one another. They are the steps, the shifts, and the mental maps in the
journey. They are the components in a "landscape of learning."

Strategies, big ideas, and models, however, are not static points in a landscape. They are dynamic movements on the part of a learner in a journey of
mathematical development. From this perspective they need to be understood as schematizing rather than as strategies, as structuring rather than as
big ideas, and as modeling rather than as models (Freudenthal 1991). Teaching needs to facilitate this development. Only then can teaching and learning be seen as interrelated—for the connected teaching/learning framework
that it is. This is the framework behind Carol's decision making.

SUMMING UP . . .

Look again at the epigraphs to this chapter. "It's the questions that drive
mathematics. Solving problems and making up new ones is the essence of
mathematical life. If mathematics is conceived apart from mathematical life,
of course it seems—dead." When mathematics is understood as mathematizing one's world—interpreting, organizing, inquiring about, and constructing meaning through a mathematical lens—it becomes creative and
alive. "The mathematician's best work is art, a high perfect art, as daring as
the most secret dreams of imagination, clear and limpid. Mathematical genius and artistic genius touch one another."

Traditionally mathematics has been taught in our schools as if it were a
dead language. It was something that past, mostly dead, mathematicians
had created—something that needed to be learned, practiced, and applied.
When the definition of mathematics shifts toward "the activity of mathematizing one's *lived* world," the constructive nature of the discipline and its
connection to problem solving become clear.

When we define mathematics in this way, and teach accordingly, children will rise to the challenge. They will grapple with mathematical ideas;
they will develop and refine strategies as they search for elegance; they will
create mathematical models as they attempt to understand and represent
their world. Because this process of mathematizing is constructive, teachers
need to walk the edge between the structure of mathematics and the devel-

opment of the learner. This edge is a journey across a landscape of learning comprising strategies, big ideas, and models. From the perspective of mathematics as mathematizing, it is the mathematical activity of the learner that ultimately matters; thus, strategies, big ideas, and models need to be understood as schematizing, structuring, and modeling. Teaching needs to be seen as inherently connected to learning.

Children, in learning to mathematize their world, will come to see mathematics as the living discipline it is, with themselves a part of a creative, constructive mathematical community, hard at work.

2 | THE LANDSCAPE OF LEARNING

It is not knowledge but the act of learning, not possession but the act of getting there, which grants the greatest enjoyment. When I have clarified and exhausted a subject, then I turn away from it, in order to go into darkness again; the never satisfied man is so strange. . . . If he has completed a structure, then it is not in order to dwell in it peacefully, but in order to begin another. I imagine the world conqueror must feel thus, who, after one kingdom is scarcely conquered, stretches out his arms for others.

—Karl Friedrich Gauss

Mathematics is not a careful march down a well-cleared highway, but a journey into a strange wilderness, where the explorers often get lost. Rigour should be a signal to the historian that maps have been made, and the real explorers have gone elsewhere.

—W. S. Anglin

DESCRIBING THE JOURNEY

Linear Frameworks

Historically, curriculum designers did not use a developmental framework like Carol's when they designed texts, nor did they see mathematics as mathematizing—as activity. They employed a teaching/learning framework based on the accumulated content of the discipline. They analyzed the structure of mathematics and delineated teaching and learning objectives along a line. Skills were assumed to accumulate eventually into concepts (Gagné 1965; Bloom et al. 1971). For example, simplistic notions of fractions were considered developmentally appropriate for early childhood if they were taught as a shaded part of a whole or with pattern blocks. Later, around third grade, the equivalence of fractions was introduced, and still later, in fifth or sixth grade, operations with fractions. Development was considered but only in relation to the content: from simple to complex skills and concepts.

Focusing only on the structure of mathematics leads to a more traditional way of teaching—one in which the teacher pushes the children toward procedures or mathematical concepts because these are the goals. In a framework like this, learning is understood to move along a line. Each lesson, each day, is geared to a different objective, a different "it." All children are expected to understand the same "it," in the same way, at the end of the lesson. They are assumed to move along the same path; if there are individual differences it is just that some children move along the path more slowly—hence, some need more time or remediation. Figure 2.1 depicts such a linear framework.

Learning Trajectories

As the reform mandated by the National Council for Teachers of Mathematics has taken hold, curriculum designers and educators have tried to develop other frameworks. Most of these approaches are based on a better understanding of children's learning and of the development of tasks that will challenge them. One important finding is that children do not all think the same way. These differences in thinking are obvious in the dialogue in Carol's classroom. Although all the children in the class worked on the submarine sandwich problem, they worked in different ways, exhibited different strategies, and acted in the environment in different mathematical ways.

Marty Simon (1995) describes a learning/teaching framework that he calls a "hypothetical learning trajectory." The learning trajectory is hypothetical because, until students are really working on a problem, we can never be sure what they will do or whether and how they will construct new interpretations, ideas, and strategies. Teachers expect their students to solve a problem in a certain way. Or, even more refined, their expectations are different for different children. Figure 2.2 depicts a hypothetical learning trajectory.

Simon uses the metaphor of a sailing voyage to explain this learning trajectory:

> You may initially plan the whole journey or only part of it. You set out sailing according to your plan. However, you must constantly adjust because of the conditions that you encounter. You continue to acquire knowledge about sailing, about the current conditions, and about the areas that you wish to visit. You change your plans with respect to the order of your destinations. You modify the length and nature of your visits as a result of interactions with people along the way. You add destinations that prior to the trip were unknown to you. The path that you travel is your [actual] trajectory. The path that you anticipate at any point is your "hypothetical trajectory." (136–37)

As this quote makes clear, teaching is a planned activity. Carol did not walk into her classroom in the morning wondering what to do. She had planned her lesson, and she knew what she expected her students to do. As the children responded, she acknowledged the differences in their thinking and in their strategies, and she adjusted her course accordingly. While she honored divergence, development, and individual differences, she also had identified landmarks along the way that grew out of her knowledge of mathematics and mathematical development. These helped her plan, question, and decide what to do next.

Over the last five years, the Mathematics in the City staff have been helping teachers like Carol develop and understand what we originally called "learning lines"—hypothetical trajectories comprising the big ideas, the mathematical models, and the strategies that children construct along the way as they grapple with key mathematical topics (addition and subtraction; multiplication and division; fractions, decimals, and percents). In conjunction with these teachers, we analyzed children's work, we looked at videotapes of lessons, and we interviewed children. We discussed the *strategies* (and their progression—the schematizing) that children used as they acted within the environment mathematically. We attempted to specify the important *big ideas* the children grappled with for each topic. And we focused on *mathematical modeling,* whereby students see, organize, and interpret their world mathematically.

Although we still believe that knowledge of models, strategies, and big ideas will enable teachers to develop a "hypothetical learning trajectory," we have stopped calling it a learning line—the term seems too linear. Learning—real learning—is messy (Duckworth 1987). We prefer instead the metaphor of a landscape.

FIGURE 2.1
Linear Framework

FIGURE 2.2
*Hypothetical Learning
Trajectory (Simon 1995)*

The big ideas, strategies, and models are important landmarks for Carol as she journeys with her students across the landscape of learning. As she designs contexts for her students to explore, her goal is to enable them to act on and within the situations mathematically and to trigger discussions about the landmarks. Carol also has horizons in mind when she plans—horizons like understanding fractions as division and equivalence of fractions to decimals and percents. As she and the children move closer to a particular horizon, landmarks shift, new ones appear.

The paths to these landmarks and horizons are not necessarily linear, and there are many such paths, not just one. As in a real landscape, the paths twist and turn; they cross one another, are often indirect. Children do not construct each of these landmark ideas and strategies in an ordered sequence. They go off in many directions as they explore, struggle to understand, and make sense of their world mathematically. Strategies do not necessarily affect the development of big ideas, or vice versa. Often constructing a big idea, like fractions as division, will affect learners' strategies for finding equivalence; but just as often "trying out" new strategies for finding equivalent fractions and then investigating why they work may help students construct insightful relationships. Ultimately, what is important is how children function in a mathematical environment (Cobb 1997)—how they mathematize.

It is not up to us, as teachers, to decide which pathways our students will use. Often, to our surprise, children will use a path we have not encountered before. That challenges us to understand the child's thinking. What is important, though, is that we help all our students reach the horizon. When we drive a car down the road, our overall attention is on the horizon. But we also see the line in the middle of the road and use it to direct the car in the right direction. Once that line is behind us, however, it no longer serves that purpose. It is the same with teaching. When a child still needs to draw and cut wholes up into equal parts to determine equivalent fractions, the teacher designs activities to support the development of fair sharing. However, when a child understands how to use ratio tables and has a variety of strategies for arriving at equivalent fractions and decimals, when it seems those landmarks have been passed, the teacher has already shifted attention to more-distant landmarks on the horizon like operating with fractions.

When we are moving across a landscape toward a horizon, the horizon seems clear. But as we near it, new objects—new landmarks—come into view. So, too, with learning. One question seemingly answered raises others. Children seem to resolve one struggle only to grapple with another. Teachers must have the horizons in mind when they plan activities, when they interact, question, and facilitate discussions. But horizons are not fixed points in the landscape; they are constantly shifting. Figure 2.3 depicts the landscape-of-learning framework.

Thinking of teaching and learning as a landscape suggests a beautiful painting. But if learners can take so many paths and the horizons are constantly shifting, how do teachers ever manage? How do we help each child make the journey and still keep in mind the responsibility we have for the class as a whole?

Carol chooses a context (field trips and submarine sandwiches) and structures fair sharing and comparing within this context because she knows that understanding fractions as division—three subs shared equally among four kids results in ¾ of a sub—is a big idea. She chooses to discuss the equivalence of ⅒ to ⅕ of ½ because she knows that understanding fractions requires understanding the relationship of parts to the whole, even when the whole changes. She is aware, as she walks around the room, of the strategies children are using—whether they draw and compare parts or use landmark fractions and their equivalents flexibly and mentally. She notices because she knows these strategies are significant in mathematical development—they represent the ways children are *schematizing* in a mathematical environment (Cobb 1997).

Word Problems vs. Truly Problematic Situations

One could argue that the use of context in mathematics teaching is not new. Certainly we all have vivid memories of word problems. Usually, however, our teachers assigned them after they had explained operations, algorithms (like invert and multiply), or rules for equivalent fractions, and we were expected to apply these procedures to the problems. In Carol's class, context is not being used for *application* at the end of a unit of instruction. It is being used at the start, for *construction*. Nor is the submarine sandwich context a trivial, camouflaged attempt to elicit "school mathematics." It is a rich, truly problematic situation that is real to the students, that allows them to generate and explore mathematical ideas, that can be entered at many levels, and that supports mathematizing.

Much reform is currently underway in schools in accordance with the new National Council for Teachers of Mathematics (NCTM) *Principles and Standards for School Mathematics* (2000), and many teachers are attempting to use problems to construct understanding rather than teach by telling. But many of the problems teachers introduce are still traditional word problems. Join us in another classroom, and we'll show you what we mean.

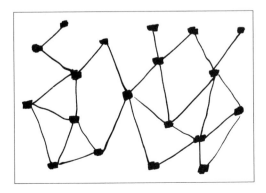

FIGURE 2.3
Landscape of Learning

Susan, a fifth-grade teacher, is reading to five children grouped around her. "'Maria went to the music store—'" She turns to the children. "Do you want me to read it, or do you want to?"

Several of the children chorus, "You."

Susan continues. "'Maria went to the music store to buy some CDs. She had twenty-four dollars with her. She spent eighteen dollars. What fractional part of her money did she spend?'" She pauses, thinks about what she has read, and then, although it is not part of the original problem, adds, "in its lowest form."

Susan begins by involving the children in solving a problem. She is not asking them to apply an algorithm for equivalent fractions, but instead she asks them to think—to solve the problem in a way that makes sense to them. She is attempting to promote construction, not application. She is clear about the mathematics (fraction as a part of a whole) she wants the children to explore, and she structures the context to support development, just as Carol did. But could Susan's context be stronger? Do the children become invested in the problem? Do they mathematize it? Or is it just a "school-type trivialized word problem"?

One of the children, Michael, starts to take the fraction bars out of a nearby bin, then puts them back, commenting, "Oh, I don't need these, easy." Other children comment that they are confused. One of these children, Josh, questions, "Just eighteen dollars? What do you mean—wasn't there tax? What do you mean lowest form?"

Susan attempts to clarify the confusion. "Look at my question. What fractional part of her money did she spend?" She pauses, then adds, "The eighteen dollars included the tax. So she spent eighteen of the twenty-four dollars. What fraction is that?"

This how-much-money scenario is one children can imagine, and in that sense it is realistic. But it is not likely to promote mathematizing. It is not likely to cause children to interpret their lived world on the basis of mathematical models. It is closed, with an expected answer of $^{18}\!/_{24}$ reduced to $^3\!/_4$—a camouflaged attempt at eliciting a fraction and reducing. Why would one ever wonder what fractional part of the twenty-four dollars was spent? In this situation, one usually only wonders how much money one has left. No wonder there is initial confusion when Susan reads the problem. In real life, there is tax, and there is no need to calculate a fraction, or to reduce. Because the children are confused, Susan must clarify. She attempts to steer the children toward the fraction that she wants them to make and reduce by rephrasing the question: "She spent eighteen of the twenty-four dollars. What fraction is that?" Unfortunately, now there is almost nothing left to solve. The context becomes irrelevant, and the children will sacrifice their own meaning making to accommodate what Susan wants.

Michael and Nora respond, "Oh, that's easy." Annie, however, remains confused.

Susan repeats the problem. "Think about it. Maria spends eighteen dollars out of the twenty-four she had. What fraction is that?"

Annie quickly says, "Oh, eighteen twenty-fourths—no."

At first Susan does not acknowledge the correctness of Annie's answer, responding, "Think about it, because you'll have to tell me how you figured it out, won't you?"

But Annie's confusion is still apparent. "I don't get it."

"Okay." Susan attempts to give Annie more time. "Josh is going on to think of another way to figure it out. Maybe the rest of you would like to find another way, too, while we give Annie more time to think about it."

Annie responds with more conviction, "Eighteen twenty-fourths— because the eighteen goes on the top and the twenty-four goes on the bottom."

This time Susan acknowledges Annie's thinking. "Okay, so now what is its lowest form? And think about how you will explain your work."

Susan is patient as she reminds Annie that she will have to explain her thinking. She does not supply an answer, nor does she acknowledge the correctness of Annie's first solution—that would stop her from thinking. To give Annie the time she needs, Susan encourages the other children to work on another strategy. But is the problem rich enough to benefit from exploring alternative strategies? What alternative strategies are there?

Teachers often confuse tools with strategies. Unifix cubes or fraction bars or paper and pencil are not different strategies. They are different tools. Representing the problem with stacks of Unifix cubes, or with fraction bars, or by drawing twenty-four dollars and circling eighteen of them are all the same mathematically. No benefit is derived by changing tools unless the new tool helps the child develop a higher level of schematizing (in this case, enables the child to construct the whole and the part and equate them to the reduced relation). Is this context rich enough for that?

Susan turns to all the children and invites them to begin a discussion. "Who would like to explain how he or she figured it out? And I would like the rest of you to listen, and if you have a question, ask."

Annie offers to begin. "If Maria had twenty-four dollars, then eighteen of that is eighteen twenty-fourths [*she counts the appropriate number of Unifix cubes as she explains*] . . . twenty-one, twenty-two, twenty-three, twenty-four. So these [*she points to a group of eighteen*] are eighteen twenty-fourths."

Susan points to the cubes and acknowledges Annie's statement. "This much is eighteen twenty-fourths of the whole." Then she turns to Michael. "Michael, you did it without manipulatives—you started to take them and then put them back. Can you explain what you did?"

"Yeah, you just take the number eighteen and put it as the numerator. The denominator is twenty-four. So I just knew it, eighteen twenty-fourths. Then you reduce. You divide each number by six and you get three fourths."

"So you just knew that the fraction eighteen twenty-fourths could be reduced to three fourths?" Susan rephrases. "Any different ways? Josh?"

Josh's strategy is similar to Annie's. He also counts, but he has drawn twenty-four dollars and circled eighteen. "There are eighteen out of twenty-four. The eighteen goes on top and the twenty-four on the bottom. Then I cut each number in half and got nine twelfths. Then I divided each by three and got three fourths."

Susan asks, "Did you just know how to reduce too, or did you use your drawing to prove it?" Josh acknowledges that he just knew. Susan then turns to Nora, who comments, "I just knew, too." Susan concludes the lesson with, "That's something that is really neat about our number system. You can reduce fractions by dividing the numerator and the denominator by the same number. It's like dividing the whole fraction by the number one. Michael, you used six sixths, and what is that equal to?"

Several children murmur, "One."

"Right. And, Josh you used two halves and then three thirds. These fractions equal one, too. Remembering that makes reducing to the lowest form easy."

Note the language the children use: "take the number eighteen and put it as the numerator," "the denominator is twenty-four," "put the eighteen on the top." They treat the problem abstractly. When a context is real and meaningful for children, their conversation relates to the context. They mathematize the situation. They talk about money, about fair sharing and portioning. There is a reason to wonder about the fractional part of the whole. There is a reason to produce equivalent fractions. They use a variety of strategies. Mathematical questions arise.

Noticing how children are thinking about a problem, noticing whether they stay grounded in the context, tells the teacher whether or not the context is a good one. When the context is a good one, the children talk about the situation. When a problem is camouflaged school mathematics, children talk about numbers abstractly; they lose sight of the problem as they try to figure out what the teacher wants.

Carol's context had the potential for genuine mathematizing as her students cut up sandwiches and attempted to determine whether the portions were fair. The situation was meaningful to them. Finding equivalent fractions in the context was critical in order to be able to compare the portions. Big ideas, like *the whole matters* (that is, $\frac{1}{5}$ of $\frac{1}{2}$ is different than $\frac{1}{5}$ of the whole sub) and the *connection of fractions to multiplication and division* (that is, three subs shared with four children produces three fourths of a sub each, because $\frac{3}{4} = 3 \times \frac{1}{4}$), surface for discussion. As the class investigated fair-sharing scenarios, patterns appeared in their data, and these patterns triggered additional explorations. In contrast, the context in traditional word problems quickly becomes unimportant; children say "put the eighteen on the top" or "eighteen twenty-fourths" rather than "three fourths of the money." And once they have an answer to the "teacher's question," they see no reason to employ alternative strategies or to inquire further.

One could argue that if Susan had asked the children to find the reduced form in Josh's drawings or Annie's cubes, more learning would have resulted. For example, Josh might have circled three out of every four dollars, or Annie might have made her cubes into four groups and shown how three of the groups was equal to the eighteen. And a discussion around the connection between these solutions might have become rich. Probably this is true. One of Susan's problems is that she too readily went to an abstract algorithm for reducing. But does the context support the development of these alternative strategies? There is no reason to find the fractional part in the first place, and even less of a reason to reduce. The context is simply a contrived one to get the children to use the mathematics Susan wants. Susan's starting point is the discipline of mathematics, a body of knowledge she knows, and she is designing problems to get children to discover it. This is distinctly different from using rich contexts to support *the development of mathematizing.*

Finding Situations for Mathematizing

If the goal of mathematics instruction is to enable children to mathematize their reality, then situations with the potential to develop the ability to mathematize need to be carefully designed (or found). To encourage children to become mathematically literate—to see themselves as mathematicians—we need to involve them in making meaning in their world mathematically.

Situations that are likely to be mathematized by learners have at least three components:

1. The potential to model the situation is built in (Freudenthal 1973). Fair-sharing scenarios, working with measurements, increasing or decreasing portions in recipes, grocery and retail store scenarios, sharing money, calculating costs and savings, following stock losses and gains, collecting data and finding ways to organize them, all have the potential to develop mathematical modeling. Using the same model over time in different situations, and reflecting on the connection, supports the development of generalization.

2. The situation allows learners to *realize what they are doing.* It can be fictitious, but children are able to experience or imagine it and are able to think and act within its parameters (Fosnot and Dolk 2001). Children, as they share submarine sandwiches in equal portions, can picture or imagine the mathematics concretely and can check the reasonableness of answers and actions. (Putting eighteen over twenty-four to make $\frac{18}{24}$ of the money makes no sense, since in this context one is not concerned with the fraction spent but with the dollar amount left.) The Dutch use the term *zich realiseren,* meaning "to realize in the sense of to picture or imagine something concretely" (van den Heuvel-Panhuizen 1996).

3. The situation prompts learners to ask questions, notice patterns, wonder, ask why and what if. Inquiry is at the heart of what it means to mathematize. Questions come from interacting with the world around us, from exploring relationships, from trying to solve problems. When the problem is "owned," it begins to come alive.

Building in Constraints

Learners' initial informal strategies are not the endpoint of instruction; they are the beginning. Teachers must transform these initial attempts into more formal and coherent mathematical strategies and models. Although peer discussions and teacher questioning can lead students to restructure their initial ideas, building constraints into the context is often a more powerful means to that end.

Both Carol and Susan choose to focus on fractions and reducing because they are important mathematical topics. But we can also build potentially realized suggestions and constraints into contexts to further support development. For example, Carol can follow her initial submarine sandwich scenario with asking her students to create a chart for the cafeteria that will ensure that everyone will always get, say, $\frac{3}{4}$ of a sub for a field trip lunch. How many subs for a group of twelve children? twenty children? How many for a group of ten children, a messier number? A context like this is likely to bring up the use of ratio tables and learner-generated rules for equivalence.

Open vs. Closed Situations

Real learning is constructive and developmental. As children attempt to make sense of a situation and its context, they interpret, organize, and model it based on the ideas or strategies they have already constructed. They schematize and structure it so that it makes sense. Piaget (1977) called this process *assimilation*, meaning "to make similar." The process of assimilation has often been misunderstood as *a taking in*. Rather, it is *an acting on*. We act on experiences when we attempt to understand them, using strategies for interpreting, inferring, and organizing. We build new ideas on old ones or reformulate old ideas into new ones.

Learners will assimilate contexts in many ways. In every classroom, developmental differences will affect perceptions and strategies. And any new ideas constructed will be directly linked in learners' minds to *their* past ideas, because they arise from reorganizing the initial ideas.

In Carol's class, the students employ any number of ideas, inquiries, and strategies. The goal is not the same for everyone every day, but there is equal opportunity for everyone to learn because the situations and their contexts are so open. The submarine sandwich scenario offers many entry points for children, from drawing the subs and cutting them to make equal parts, to determining what to call pieces of pieces ($\frac{1}{5}$ of $\frac{1}{2}$, for example), to working with landmark fractions for comparison, to exploring fractions as common fractions or as the sum of unit fractions. Carol varies her questions to stretch and support individual children's learning.

Closed situations have only one possible strategy. Everyone is supposed to solve the problem in the same way, and learners are either successful or unsuccessful—they either get it or they don't. Open situations, crafted sophisticatedly with a didactical use of context, allow for and support developmental differences, and thus can facilitate mathematical development for everyone.

Word Problems vs. Context Problems

Word problems on the surface appear to offer many possible strategies by which to arrive at a solution. But because they are often designed with little context, they are usually nothing more than superficial, camouflaged attempts to get children to do the procedures teachers want them to do—procedures that have little to do with genuine mathematizing. And they often cause students to answer them in ways that fail to take account of the reality of the situations described (Verschaffel et al. 2000). Context problems, on the other hand, are connected as closely as possible to children's lives, rather than to "school mathematics." They are designed to anticipate and develop children's mathematical modeling of the real world. Thus, they encourage learners to invent genuine diverse solutions. In addition, context problems have built-in constraints in an attempt to support and stretch initial mathematizing. In this sense, their purpose is to promote the *development* of mathematizing. But is even this enough?

Context-Based Investigations and Inquiries

If genuine mathematizing involves setting up relationships, searching for patterns, constructing models, and proposing conjectures and proving them, then context must be used in a way that simultaneously involves children in problem solving *and* problem posing. Carol could simply have asked her students to figure out how much of a sub each child would get if four children were given three subs to share. This is a real situation, one that children could mathematize in many ways because they might divide the subs differently. They could count; they could explore naming pieces of pieces. But would children have noticed the pattern that Jennifer and John noticed? Would Jackie and Ernie have come up with their elegant comparison strategy? Would Michael, Gabrielle, and Ashleigh have constructed the equivalence of the summed unit fractions to common fractions? Would the problem be messy enough to support inquiry?

To allow the students to notice patterns, the situation and its context had to be open enough that patterns in data would appear. Piaget (1977) argued that setting up correspondences by learners is the beginning of the development of an understanding of relationships. Constructing a connection, a pattern, or a correspondence between objects fosters reflection. Learners begin to wonder why; they want to explain and understand the connections they notice. By building a problem with four situations, rather than one, and by asking her students to compare them, Carol opens the situation to become a genuine investigation rather than a problem, and the children can begin to construct relationships from the patterns they notice. But still this is not enough.

Carol must also facilitate the students' questions. As they raise inquiries, Carol gets excited along with them and deliberately gets them to discuss their ideas. She supports their inquiries by giving them the time and the materials to pursue them. If she had not facilitated this aspect of mathematizing—the problem posing—but instead had relied on a series of context problems to be solved (even when carefully structured day by day), she would not have developed in the children the ability to mathematize *their* lived world. Some children would have been lost along the way as the class as a whole moved from activity to activity. Instead, by using context-based *investigations* and by facilitating *inquiry* in relation to them, Carol involves her children in genuine mathematizing, in being young mathematicians at work.

TURNING CLASSROOMS INTO MATHEMATICAL COMMUNITIES

Knowing the difference between word problems, context problems, investigations, and inquiries, and knowing how to keep them open, helps Carol support each child. Understanding how to mold contexts is an important didactical tool for stretching each child. But understanding the role of context is not enough. Carol also makes her classroom a community in which her students can investigate and share with one another. Developing a community that supports risk taking and mathematical discussions is another critical pedagogical component for fostering real investigations and inquiries— real mathematizing.

The Edge Between the Individual and the Community

Teaching has two important and very different phases. At home, at night, we prepare for the next day. We replay the day just past, remembering the successes, evaluating the inquiries, celebrating the insights some of the children had, recalling the stumbling blocks and the struggles—all from the perspective of mathematical development, with a sense of the landscape of learning. Although our reflections begin with individual children, as we plan we shift our attention to the community—the whole class. Our intent is to keep everyone in the community moving—to move the community as a whole across the landscape toward the horizon. No matter what path a child is on, no matter where on that path the child is, we want to move that child closer to the horizon. Fortunately, we do not need to plan separate lessons for each child—nor could we. Instead we can focus on the community, thinking of contexts and situations that will be likely to move the community as a whole closer to the horizon. To that end, our lessons must be open and rich enough that each community member can enter them and be challenged.

The next day, in class, our role changes dramatically. We become a member of the community. We listen to and interact with the children. We try to understand what each child is thinking. We decide whether to ask for clarification. We pose questions that will cause children to think. We are intrigued with individual inquiries and solutions. We think about how members of the community can help one another, how they can build their ideas upon others' ideas. The night before, we are curriculum designers—designing the environment for the community. In class, we are researchers and guides. We journey with the children.

Therein lies our duality: we are community members, yet we plan for the community. We facilitate conversation around mathematical ideas and strategies for the community to consider. But, as a member of the community, we help develop the norms of what it means to prove something, of what counts as a solution, or a conjecture. We walk the edge between the community and the individual.

Facilitating Dialogue

Turning a classroom of between twenty and thirty individuals into a community is not easy: it's a structure very different from the classrooms most of us attended. Traditionally, dialogue in a classroom bounced from teacher to student, back to the teacher, then to another student. The teacher was there to question and give feedback. She stood at the front of the classroom; the learners were spread out in front of her.

In a "community of discourse" (Fosnot 1989), participants speak with one another. They ask questions of one another and comment on one another's ideas. They defend their ideas to the community, not just to the teacher. Ideas are accepted in the community insofar as they are agreed upon as shared and not disproved. The community develops its own norms for what it means to prove one's argument, for what stands as a mathematical problem, for how data get collected, represented, and shared. As a member of the community (but walking the edge), the teacher facilitates, monitors, and at times provides counterexamples and/or highlights connections to ensure that this dialogue supports genuine mathematical learning.

Several strategies can be helpful. After a student shares an idea, we can ask, *How many of you understand this point well enough to rephrase it in your own words?* (Or, as Carol did, "Who understands and can put in their own words where this group got the answer one tenth?") The students' responses tell us not only how many of them appear to understand but also *how* they understand, how they are schematizing, structuring, and modeling. Discussion cannot happen if the community is not considering the speaker's thinking. Because construction, not transmission, lies at the heart of learning, everyone is responsible for thinking about and commenting on one another's ideas. After several children have paraphrased an idea and we are confident that most students are participating, we can ask follow-up questions: *Does anyone have a question? Who agrees? Who disagrees? Does anyone have a different idea or a different way of thinking about it?* Questions like these keep the dialogue bouncing from student to student, from community member to community member.

Structuring Math Workshop

Investigations

When classrooms are workshops—when learners are inquiring, investigating, and constructing—there is already a feeling of community. In workshops learners talk with one another, ask one another questions, collaborate, prove and communicate their thinking to one another. The heart of math workshop is this: investigations are ongoing, and teachers try to find situations and structure contexts that will enable children to mathematize their lives—that will move the community toward the horizon. Children have the opportunity to explore, to pursue inquiries, and to model and solve problems in their own creative ways. Searching for patterns, raising questions, and constructing one's own models, ideas, and strategies are the primary goals of a math workshop. The classroom becomes a community of learners engaged in activity, discourse, and reflection.

Math Congress

After investigating and writing up solutions and conjectures, the community convenes for a "math congress." This is more than just a whole-group share. The congress continues the work of helping children become mathematicians in a mathematics community. Mathematicians communicate their ideas, solutions, problems, proofs, and conjectures to one another. In fact, mathematical ideas are held as "truth" only insofar as the mathematical community accepts them as true.

In a math congress, learners—young mathematicians at work—defend their thinking. Out of the congress come ideas and strategies that form the emerging discipline of mathematics in the classroom. The sociocultural aspects of this emerging discipline are directly connected to the community. What holds up as a proof, as data, as a convincing argument? What counts as a beautiful idea or an efficient strategy? How will ideas be symbolized? What is mathematical language? What does it mean to talk about mathematics? What tools count as mathematical tools? What makes a good mathematical question? What serves as a conjecture? All of these questions get answered in the interactions of the community. The answers arise from the sociocultural norms and mores that develop (Cobb 1996; Yackel 2001).

Once again we as teachers are on the edge. We must walk the line between the structure and the development of mathematics, and between the individual and the community. As we facilitate discussions, as we decide which ideas to focus on, we develop the community's norms and mores with regard to mathematics, and we stretch and support individual learners. We move the community toward the horizon, *and* we enable individuals to travel their own path.

We can structure math congresses in many ways. If we want to focus on a big idea or illuminate mathematical modeling, we can bring out the connections between different solutions and strategies. If we want to support the progressive development of strategies, we can direct the discussion from less efficient to more efficient solutions. Our goal is always to develop mathematizing—to promote shifts in thinking, to help learners develop mental maps. We focus on the community's journey, yet we work toward each student's construction of meaning.

Minilessons

A description of math workshop would not be complete without a few words about minilessons. Often we may wish to highlight a computational strategy, share a problem-solving approach, or discuss a historical proof. A ten-minute minilesson at the start of math workshop is a great way to do so. (Chapter 7 provides examples of many minilessons teachers have presented to develop mental math computation strategies.) In a minilesson, we as teachers take a more explicit role in bringing ideas and strategies to the surface. But once again we walk the edge. We put forth ideas for the community to consider, but we must allow individuals to construct their own meaning.

SUMMING UP . . .

Learning and teaching are interrelated; one does not occur without the other. Genuine learning is not linear. It is messy, arrived at by many paths, and characterized by different-size steps and shifts in direction. Genuine teaching is directed toward landmarks and horizons. The first epigraph to this chapter is a statement by the great mathematician Karl Gauss: "It is not knowledge but the act of learning, not possession but the act of getting there, which grants the greatest enjoyment." As we learn, we construct. We near the horizon only to have new landmarks appear. As W. S. Anglin reminds us, "Mathematics is not a careful march down a well-cleared highway, but a journey."

Because learning is not linear, teaching cannot be either. If we as teachers have a deep knowledge of the landscape of learning—the big ideas, the strategies, and the models that characterize the journey—we can build contexts that develop children's ability to mathematize. By opening up situations into investigations and facilitating inquiry, we can support children's journeys along many paths.

But we need to walk the line between supporting individuals and planning for the community. Development of the class as a community is critical. In a community, trust and respect are shared by everyone. Traditionally, respect was reserved for the teacher: the teacher spoke, learners listened, and the teacher always had the last word. For a community to function well, all members must respect one another. Everyone's ideas deserve attention, and each person must be trusted to be responsible for the task at hand. Everyone must be trusted to be able to learn. In the beginning of the year, teachers need to work hard establishing routines and structures for math workshop. The learners in their charge must be led to trust that their ideas count, that their peers and the teacher really care about their thinking, that they will be given the time to explore different strategies and pursue their inquiries, that their questions and insights matter.

But community cannot be divorced from content. Mathematicians talk about mathematical ideas, not feelings or rules of behavior. They respect one another for the mathematical ideas they bring to the discussion. Learners, no matter how young, know when they are really being listened to. They know when they are learning and when they are not. They know when what they are doing is interesting, when it matters, and when it is simply about pleasing the teacher. When intriguing contexts are being explored and mathematical big ideas are being grappled with, engagement is high. Children can be mathematicians when teachers give them a chance to mathematize *their* reality, and trust that they can.

3 | EQUIVALENCE ON THE HORIZON

Sesostris . . . made a division of the soil of Egypt among the inhabitants. . . . If the river carried away any portion of a man's lot, the king sent persons to examine, and determine by measurement the exact extent of the loss.

—Heroclitus

Mathematics was born and nurtured in a cultural environment. Without the perspective the cultural background affords, a proper appreciation of the content and state of present-day mathematics is hardly possible.

—R. L. Wilder

Nothing is more important than to see the sources of invention, which are in my opinion more interesting than the inventions themselves.

—G. W. Leibniz

FAIR SHARING: THE HISTORICAL ROOTS OF EQUIVALENCE

Early Number Systems

It is easy to see why humans invented number systems. How do we comprehend and communicate "how many"? Although the eye can often perceive five or fewer objects as a whole, amounts larger than this must be counted or decomposed into smaller amounts that can be subitized and then added. In fact, if our fingers were to be cut off and placed in front of us on a table, we would not be able to see, at a glance, if one had been lost (Guedj 1996). Because we cannot "see" large quantities as a whole but instead must operate on them to determine quantity, humans constructed ways to represent amounts symbolically and to communicate these amounts to one another: we invented numerals and operations.

Over time and across cultures, many oral and written systems emerged. Within early number systems, although new symbols were invented to show quantities of groups rather than single units, the number of shapes drawn was usually one to one, either units or number of groups. And different symbols were used for different-size groups. For example, the Mayans of the Yucatán used a bar to equal five and a dot to represent units. They wrote 19 with three bars and four dots. They grouped by twenties, thus 80 would be written as four twenties. Ancient Egyptians used lines to represent ones, a basket handle to represent tens, a coiled rope to represent hundreds, and a lotus flower blooming on its stalk to represent thousands. They wrote 19 with one basket handle and nine lines (Fosnot and Dolk 2001). These were cumbersome systems for calculating and for writing large numbers, and eventually these systems were replaced by the development of the Hindu-Arabic place value system we use now.

But why did humans invent fractions? What problems led humans to require them? People of the Stone Age seem to have had no use for fractions. The notion of a rational number developed relatively late in the history of humankind and was not in general closely related to the development of a system of integers. And decimals were the product of the modern age in mathematics, rather than of an ancient period (Boyer 1991).

Unit Fractions

The more advanced cultures during the Bronze Age, like the Mayans and the Egyptians, dealt with problems that required the representation of ratios and fractional amounts. Since then, through time and across diverse cultures, human beings have been very inventive in finding ways to represent equivalence for fractional amounts.

In ancient Egypt, fair-sharing situations brought about the use of unit fractions—fractions in which the numerator is one. For example, Egyptians drew a loaf over eight tallies to represent one loaf of bread for eight people. Common fractions such as $\frac{3}{5}$ were not used, the exception being $\frac{2}{3}$—and this was considered a special number, equivalent to $\frac{1}{2} + \frac{1}{6}$. Of course situations such as three loaves for five people occurred but would be represented not as $\frac{3}{5}$ but with the unit fractions of $\frac{1}{3} + \frac{1}{5} + \frac{1}{15}$. Within a context of fair sharing, this makes perfect sense. Imagine the first two loaves cut into thirds, and the last loaf cut into fifths. These pieces can be shared easily by the five people. One third of the second loaf is left and it must be cut into fifths. This produces $\frac{1}{15}$ of a loaf more for each person. (See Figure 3.1.)

It has been suggested that the unit fractions used were dictated by the Egyptian preference for fractions derived from the "natural" fractions $\frac{1}{2}$, $\frac{1}{3}$, and $\frac{2}{3}$ and by successive halving (Boyer 1991). Try another situation: two loaves for fifteen people. To express $\frac{2}{15}$ as a sum of unit fractions, start by taking half of each loaf. Then, $\frac{1}{5}$ of $\frac{1}{2}$ (five slices out of each of three halves) produces the first fifteen slices. The last half must be divided into fifteen slices, producing $\frac{1}{30}$ of a loaf more for each person. Thus for ancient Egyptians, two loaves shared with fifteen people was represented as $\frac{1}{10} + \frac{1}{30}$. (See Figure 3.2.) To calculate they used a table of unit fractions that had been written down by the scribe Ahmes between 1680 and 1620 B.C.

Today we think of $\frac{6}{10}$ as itself a rational number, as .6, as 60 percent, and as a reducible fraction (to $\frac{3}{5}$). How did these systems of equivalence evolve? What forms of equivalence did other cultures use?

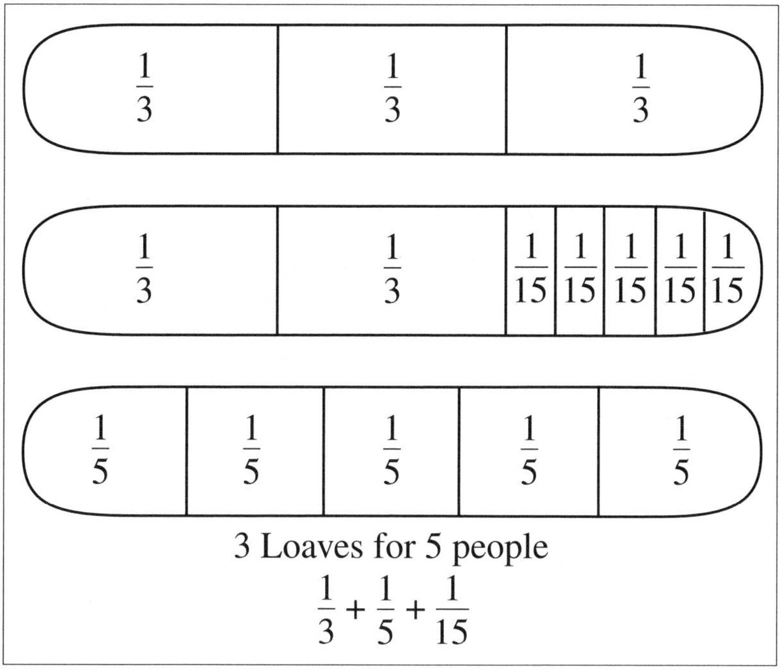

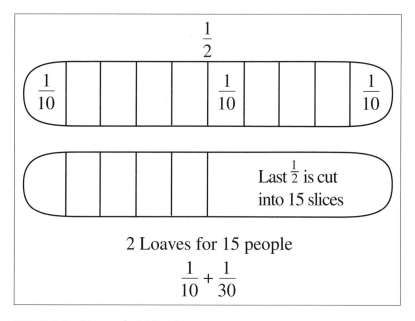

FIGURE 3.1   *3 Loaves for 5 People*

FIGURE 3.2   *2 Loaves for 15 People*

Sexagesimals

The Babylonians lived near Egypt, in Mesopotamia, a fertile plain between the Tigris and Euphrates Rivers in Africa. Very early on (3500 B.C. or so), this region had been the center of the advanced Sumerian civilization, which built cities and supported the people in them with irrigation systems, a legal system, an administrative system, and even a postal service. Writing developed, and counting was based on a sexagesimal system—that is, one based on powers of sixty. Around 2300 B.C. the Akkadians invaded the area and for some time the culture of the Akkadians mixed with the culture of the Sumerians. The Akkadians invented the abacus as a tool for counting, and they developed somewhat clumsy methods of arithmetic, with addition, subtraction, multiplication, and division all playing a part. The Sumerians, however, revolted against Akkadian rule and by 2100 B.C. they were back in control. Over time the Babylonian civilization replaced that of the Sumerians. The Babylonians used the positional number system with a base of sixty to represent fractions, particularly in measurement contexts. For example, they divided the day into twenty-four hours, each hour into sixty minutes, each minute into sixty seconds. This form of time measurement has survived for four thousand years. The designation 5h 25′ 30″ (five hours, twenty-five minutes, thirty seconds) implies a mixed number with two sexagesimal fractions—$5 \, ^{25}/_{60} \, ^{30}/_{3600}$. The Babylonians also developed a table for sexagesimals: $\frac{1}{2}$ is equivalent to .30, $\frac{1}{3}$ is equivalent to .20, etc. (They did not use the decimal point or the bar for fractions as we are doing here, but their table of equivalence was remarkable.)

The Rise of Common Fractions

There was some use of common fractions by the Greeks (circa 300 B.C.) to express ratios and proportions in measurements and geometry. (See, for example, the ratio of the length of line segment AB to line segment AC, shown in Figure 3.3.) They also had ways to figure out equivalent ratios. Eudoxus wrote:

> Magnitudes are said to be in the same ratio, the first to the second and the third to the fourth, when if any equimultiples whatever be taken of the first and the third, and any equimultiples whatever of the second and fourth, the former equimultiples alike exceed, are alike equal to, or are alike less than the latter equimultiples taken in corresponding order. (Heath 1981, vol. 2, p. 114, cited in Boyer 1991)

This rather verbose definition of equality of ratios, simply put, is not unlike the process of cross-multiplication that is used today for fractions:

$a/b = c/d$ if and only if $ad = bc$. But although the Greeks were fascinated by ratios, they continued in general to prefer unit fraction equivalences for computation. And most of their measurements were written in sexagesimal forms. They simply subdivided units of length, weight, and money so effectively that they could calculate in terms of integral multiples: sixty had far more factors than ten and thus many more subdivisions could occur with a measurement system based on sixty than with one based on ten.

The Rise of Decimal Fractions

In contrast, early Chinese civilizations (also circa 300 B.C.) used the abacus with a base-ten system but with no zero. Here an early form of decimal fractions appeared—$\frac{1}{10}$, $\frac{3}{10}$, $\frac{1}{100}$, etc.—as a result of using the abacus. The Chinese were also familiar with operations on common fractions: they knew how to find common denominators. Interestingly, they referred to the numerator as the "son" and the denominator as the "mother" and developed rules for manipulating fractions using a yin/yang analogy. Because most calculations were carried out on the abacus, however, common fractions were usually transformed into decimal fractions. For example, $\frac{3}{5}$ would be handled on the abacus as six out of ten.

EXPANDING COMMERCIAL MARKETS AS A CONTEXT

In spite of these few precursors to our current use of fractions and decimals, it took almost fifteen hundred years more before the forms of fractions and decimals as we know them evolved. In general, sexagesimals and unit frac-

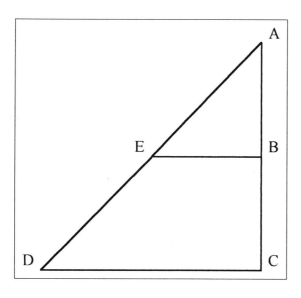

FIGURE 3.3
*Geometrical
Measurement Context
Where Greeks Employed
Common Fractions as
Ratios: AB/AC*

tions were the predominant methods used in representing and calculating fractional amounts until the Middle Ages, and it was really well into the Renaissance period before they were replaced with decimal and common fraction notations. The bar notation for fractions as we know it first appeared in Arabia with the invention of the Hindu-Arabic system and was made popular in a book by Leonardo of Pisa (circa 1180–1250), better known as Fibonnaci. The book, *Liber Abaci* (*Book of the Abacus*), opens with the idea that geometry and arithmetic are connected. Rather than discussing the use of the abacus however, as one might be led to expect from the title, Fibonnaci describes the Hindu-Arabic number system (digits 1–9 and 0) and its importance for problems in commercial transactions. Interestingly, he did not discuss a decimal system.

One of the ironies of history is that the chief advantage of positional notation—its applicability to fractions—almost entirely escaped the users of the Hindu-Arabic numerals for the first thousand years of their existence (Boyer 1991). Instead Fibonnaci used three types of fractions (unit, common, and sexagesimal) in connection with problems of the following type: *If 1 solidus imperial, which is 12 deniers imperial, is sold for 31 deniers Pisan, how many deniers Pisan should one obtain for 11 deniers imperial?* With an algorithm, he showed how to produce the answer of $\frac{5}{12}$ 28. Fibonacci customarily placed the fractional part or parts of a mixed number before the integral part; we would write this $28\frac{5}{12}$. Instead of writing $11\frac{5}{6}$, he wrote $\frac{1}{3}\frac{1}{2}11$, with the juxtaposition of unit fractions and integers implying addition (Boyer 1991). Analogously, in another of the many problems on monetary conversion in *Liber Abaci*, he writes that if $\frac{1}{4}\frac{2}{3}$ of a rotulus is worth $\frac{1}{7}\frac{1}{6}\frac{2}{5}$ of a bizantium, then $\frac{1\ 4\ 7}{8\ 9\ 10}$ of a bizantium is worth $\frac{3\ 8\ 83\ 11}{4\ 10\ 149\ 12}$ of a rotulus where, in the odd notation Fibonacci used, $\frac{1\ 4\ 7}{8\ 9\ 10}$ means $1/(8 \times 9 \times 10) + 4/(9 \times 10) + 7/10$. Imagine the merchants of the Middle Ages operating with such a system!

As commercialism took hold in the Renaissance and merchants became proficient in the use of the Hindu-Arabic system, decimal notation began to emerge. Francoise Viete (1540–1603), a member of Henry IV's council, proclaimed:

> Sexagesimals and sixties are to be used sparingly or never in mathematics, and thousandths and thousands, hundredths and hundreds, tenths and tens, and similar progressions, ascending and descending, are to be used frequently or exclusively. (in Boyer 1991, p. 303)

A lover of mathematics himself, he devoted much of his spare time to reconfiguring tables and computations in use at that time to decimal fractions. The use of a decimal point followed soon after and is usually attributed to either Magini or Clavius, both friends of the astronomer Kepler.

Today, for ratio problems such as those encountered in the marketplace, we just multiply and divide, and probably with the calculator! And given that our current money system is based on decimals, many ratio problems are easy to do even mentally. For example: *Which is the better buy, 20 cans of cat food for $23, or 12 cans for $15?* Probably you can think of several quick, efficient ways to compare these ratios.

Why did it take humans so long to work out simple representations for ratios and strategies for equivalence? It is one thing to understand that the numerical symbol (such as 6) can be used to represent amounts (six things or six groups)—this idea by itself was huge when it was first constructed. But fractions are ratios and proportions (three loaves for five people); they represent the operations of multiplication and division (3 divided by 5 and 3 times $\frac{1}{5}$); they are relations on relations ($a/b = c/d$ if and only if $ad = bc$). They are the result of treating numbers in relation to each other to form new numbers. They are the result of forming new ways to represent rational amounts and proving that many forms are equivalent even though they don't look alike.

Mathematical ideas develop as humans grapple with problems they encounter (and pose) as they interact within their cultural communities. The ideas previously constructed in the culture, the tools of the culture, and the number systems prevalent all have an effect on the evolution of new ideas. And as cultures expand, merge with others, and interact, new problems as well as new insights continue to facilitate evolution. Mathematizing is progressive. Humans build ideas, one upon another, often negating or reformulating previous ones. They do not discover them; they invent them as they mathematize their lived worlds. By analyzing the historical origins we can gain insights into the landscape of learning. As we work with the young mathematicians in our classrooms, we can recognize the landmarks as we pass them and view what is to come.

CHILDREN'S STRATEGIES FOR EQUIVALENCE

In Chapter 1, we witnessed Carol Mosesson's students inventing ways to deal with fair-sharing situations. We saw them construct both unit fractions and common fractions; they grappled with how multiplication and division are connected to fractions; they worked out strategies for equivalence. These are not trivial ideas or strategies. They took human beings centuries to develop!

Let's visit another classroom, this time grade 6, as students work on the problem of which cat food is the best buy (20 for $23 or 12 for $15). Joel Spengler, their teacher, has asked the children to help him decide which is the best buy. He has just bought a new kitten and he has seen two sale prices (in two different stores, Maria's and Bob's) for special kitten food.

Two girls, Helaina and Lucy, are working together with large paper and markers. "Let's pretend it's one dollar a can at both places," Helaina suggests as a way to begin. "That leaves three dollars each time."

"So we know it's a little more than one dollar a can." Lucy concludes.

"But how much more, that's the problem!" Helaina sighs. The girls are struggling with a way to establish equivalence so that a comparison can be made. What will they use as a whole? What would be a good unit of comparison?

"Why don't we just divide?" Lucy suggests. "Let's see how much it is exactly for each can." They decide to compare units—the cost of one can at each store. They divide 15 by 12 and get $1\frac{1}{4}$. "That's a dollar and twenty-five cents," comments Lucy. "A quarter is twenty-five cents." Next they divide 23 by 20 and get $1\frac{3}{20}$. "So how much money is that?" Lucy asks. Now they have a new problem, how to determine the decimal equivalent.

Chloe and Josephine, at the far end of the room, are working on the same problem, although they began differently. They started with an equivalence of $\frac{15}{12}$ to $\frac{5}{4}\frac{5}{4}\frac{5}{4}$, commenting, "There's three groups of five dollars for four cans. If we divide each of these numbers," pointing to the 15 and the 12, "we get the cost of four cans, five dollars." At first they thought they would find the cost of four cans at Maria's shop and compare that to the cost of four cans at Bob's, but this proved too difficult for them. The latter numbers do not break up as nicely.

"So let's find the cost of one can," Chloe suggests. Their strategy is not division, however, like Lucy and Helaina's. They make unit fraction equivalents. Chloe continues, "Five fourths is the same as four fourths plus one fourth, or one plus one fourth, so that's one can for a dollar-twenty-five. Now, how should we do twenty-three twentieths?"

Both girls at first are puzzled.

"I have an idea," Josephine offers. "It's one and three twentieths, right?" Chloe nods in agreement. This part was easy for her to see too, but she wonders what Josephine will do next. "Three twentieths is the same as one twentieth plus one twentieth plus one twentieth." Once again Chloe nods in agreement. "Okay," Josephine announces, "so what is one twentieth of a dollar?"

Chloe thinks for a brief moment and then offers, "Five cents?"

"Right," Josephine agrees emphatically. "So times three, that's fifteen cents!"

"Oh cool," Chloe comments, impressed with their results. "So that's a better deal. It's a dollar-fifteen a can in that store."

All four girls have approached the problem by establishing a comparison per unit can. But the strategy for doing so within each group is different. Lucy and Helaina divide to find the cost of each unit (see Figure 3.4). Josephine and Chloe have made equivalent fractions by simplifying and finding unit fractions (see Figure 3.5).

Dylan and Tristan employ yet another strategy; they construct a ratio table (see Figure 3.6). Using their ratio table, they are able to combine amounts to establish equivalence. As they ponder which amount of units to compare (cost of a certain number of cans), they hit on the brilliant idea of using a common multiple, "Hey, we could try sixty cans!" Dylan suggests. "Both twelve and twenty go into sixty equally." They add 60 to their ratio table, finding that the cost at Maria's will be $69 while the cost of that amount at Bob's will be $75.

The classroom is a community of young mathematicians at work. As such, several different approaches have been taken to establish equivalence; several different forms of mathematizing are visible. Some are reminiscent of Babylonian unit fractions; others employ ratio tables and common multiples; still others show evidence of division. Because the classroom is a community comprising individuals, it is a rich arena of diversity. Equivalence is on the horizon as Joel thinks about where he is going, but children are at different landmarks in the journey. Joel uses this fact to his advantage as he convenes a math congress.

Math Congress

"Yesterday, as you were investigating which store had the 'best buy' on cat food, I noticed several strategies and I would like to talk about those today. Helaina and Lucy . . . would you begin and tell us what you did?"

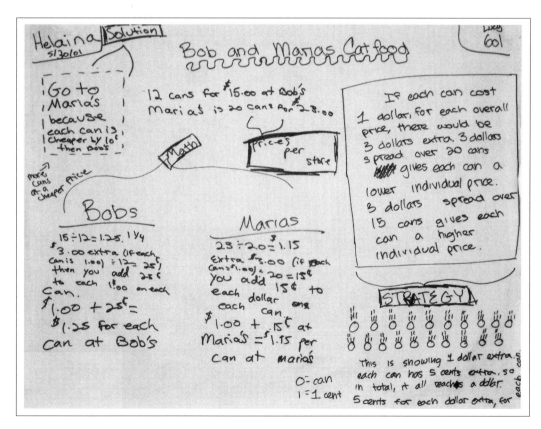

FIGURE 3.4 *Helaina and Lucy's Strategy*

"We noticed that if we gave one dollar to each can, at each store we would have three dollars left," Helaina begins. "Three divided by twelve was twenty-five cents. So at Bob's the cat food can costs $1.25."

Lucy finishes the explanation, "At Maria's we had three dollars left and we realized that was a nickel out of each dollar, since there are twenty nickels in a dollar . . . that's fifteen cents! So it was $1.15."

"Who can explain the strategy Helaina and Lucy used?" Joel checks for understanding by turning to the community. Rather than explaining himself, he makes the students responsible for communicating about and un-

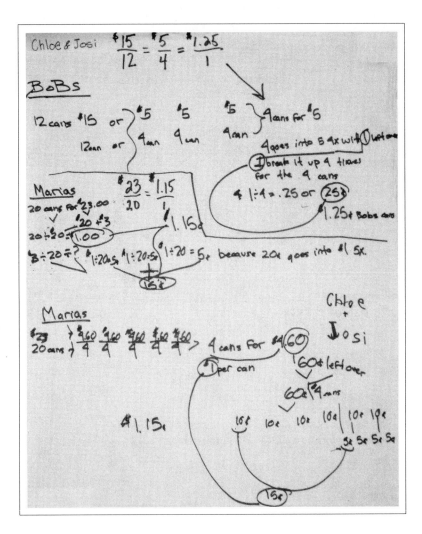

FIGURE 3.5 *Chloe and Josi's Strategy*

derstanding each other's work. He does this because as the students explain their thinking to each other, they are thinking more deeply about the mathematics and they are learning how to communicate mathematical ideas to each other. After it appears that Helaina and Lucy's strategy is understood, Joel turns to Tristan and Dylan and asks them to share their strategy. They have used a ratio table.

"We started by halving," Dylan explains. "If twelve cans cost $15, then six cans would cost $7.50, and three cans would cost $3.75. We couldn't

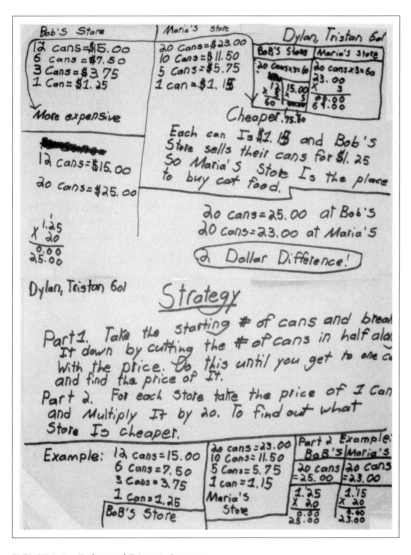

FIGURE 3.6   *Dylan and Tristan's Strategy*

halve again because that would give us one and one half cans. So we took a third, and we got the cost of one can, $1.25. Then we did the same thing with Maria's. If twenty cans cost $23, then ten cans cost $11.50. That means five cans cost $5.75, and one can costs $1.15."

Some discussion ensues as the children all work to understand how Dylan and Tristan arrived at their ratios. When agreement is reached, Joel suggests that he will keep track of all the different ratios in a T chart and he draws the charts in Figure 3.7.

"Are there other numbers we could have used, too?" Joel turns to Chloe and Josephine. "What did you two do?"

"We looked for a common multiple, no a factor. We picked four because it went into twenty cans evenly and into twelve cans evenly," Chloe explains. "At Maria's there were twenty cans. That's five groups of four. So every four cans cost $4.60. At Bob's there were twelve cans. That's three groups of four. So every four cans there cost $5."

Joel adds these ratios to the T chart as well. "So let me see, are we saying that all of these are equivalent?" Above the charts he writes $^{15}/_{12} = \$7.50/6$. "Are these two equivalent? Take thirty seconds and discuss this with the person sitting next to you." In order to ensure that each student is actively thinking about the equivalence, Joel requests "pair talk" instead of whole-class talk. By doing so he is guaranteed that each student is involved in considering the big idea at hand—equivalence. After listening in on a few conversations he resumes with whole-class discussion. "Ilit? What did you and your partner discuss?"

"We thought they were equivalent," Ilit offers, "because fifteen divided by two equals 7.50. It's half the numerator. And the denominator . . . twelve divided by two, is six. That's half, too."

"Do you all agree with Ilit? Does anyone want to add anything? Kevin?"

"I agree with Ilit. If you do the same thing to both the numerator and the denominator, they are equivalent."

"Do you all agree? If we do the same thing to the cans as to the dollars, they are equivalent?" Joel stays within the context to enable his students to realize what they are doing. As he looks at his students' faces, they all seem to be agreeing and so he goes on. "And so can I add these fractions, too?"

Bob's		Maria's	
12 cans	$15.00	20 cans	$23.00
6 cans	$ 7.50	10 cans	$11.50
3 cans	$ 3.75	5 cans	$ 5.75
1 can	$ 1.25	1 can	$ 1.15

FIGURE 3.7 *Joel's T chart*

Joel adds the other ratios from the T chart to his equation. Now he has written on the chalkboard $^{15}\!/_{12} = {}^{7.50}\!/_6 = {}^{3.75}\!/_3 = {}^{1.25}\!/_1 = {}^5\!/_4$.

"Yes," several students offer verbal agreement. Others nod affirmatively.

"And so for Maria's, can I do the same thing here?" Joel writes $^{\$23}\!/_{20} = {}^{\$11.50}\!/_{10} = {}^{\$5.75}\!/_5 = {}^{\$1.15}\!/_1 = {}^{\$4.60}\!/_4$. Once again his students nod affirmatively so Joel continues to develop more equivalences, "Andres and Zach . . . you guys used sixty cans to compare. Can you explain why?"

"It was a common multiple. We multiplied twenty by three, and twelve by five."

Joel adds $^2\!/_{60}$ to each equation as Andres and Zach explain. But rather than allowing them to continue to explain how they figured the cost of sixty cans at each store, he interrupts them and once again engages everyone in "pair talk." He wants everyone involved in calculating the equivalent fractions. "So what do you think Andres and Zach did? If I buy sixty cans at each store . . . take a minute and turn to the person next to you and discuss how much sixty cans would cost at each store."

After listening to a few conversations, Joel notes that his students appear to be able to easily determine the numerator. He asks Zev to explain what most students have discussed. "Zev?"

"$23.00 for twenty cans so $69.00 for sixty cans. It's just times three because the cans are times three."

"And Corinne . . . how about Bob's store?" Joel brings another voice into the conversation.

"We did . . . I think this is right. Since you multiplied twelve by five to get sixty, you have to multiply fifteen by five, too. So we got seventy-five dollars over sixty cans."

Joel adds these equivalent fractions to his equations and asks, "So these are all equivalent? Whatever we do to the numerator, we have to do to the denominator?"

Noting agreement once again, Joel returns to the T chart and encourages them to use it as a ratio table—as a tool. "Is there another number of cans here that we could also compare?" Once again Joel resumes "pair talk" and then asks Ga-yen to share. Each time he uses "pair talk" he brings more voices to the conversation. "Ga-yen . . . would you describe what you and Felisha discussed?"

"We thought that if you divided seventy-five by two, and sixty by two, you would get another equivalent ratio."

"And what did you get?" Joel inquires further.

"$37.50 for thirty cans."

"And for Maria's store? What would thirty cans cost there? Jeremy?"

"34.50 . . . that's half of sixty-nine."

"And are there other numbers of cans we could compare? . . . Chloe?"

Chloe has used the friendly number ten. "It's $11.50 for ten cans so it's three times that . . . $34.50, for thirty cans," she explains with confidence.

"And what about twenty cans?" Joel continues engaging them in working with the ratio table. "Could we figure the cost of that amount at each store? . . . Carol?"

"That's double the cost of ten. And then the cost of twenty cans and the cost of ten cans could be added to determine the cost of thirty cans," Carol exclaims with excitement.

Now Veronica's hand is up and Joel smiles as she offers her insights, "It's like . . . we could also use twenty thirtieths and multiply it by one and a half over one and a half . . . that's the same as adding the cost of twenty and the cost of ten!"

Joel's students have worked out many ways to determine and prove equivalence. They are using the ratio table as a tool; they are establishing equivalence by multiplying or dividing the numerator and denominator by the same amount—by multiplying or dividing the original fraction by one. They are able to determine unit equivalences and common fractions. They are constructing and representing ideas about fractions that took humans centuries!

Extending Equivalence to Decimals and Percents

Joel's students are able to make decimal and fraction equivalents. But that is because they are within the context of money. Since our money system is decimal-based, it serves as a wonderful context in which to develop landmark equivalents (.5, .50, 50%; 10%, .10, .1; .25, 25%; etc.). Generalizing to other decimal and percent equivalents, however, is important and necessary. What contexts are helpful here?

Liza Hernandez developed a patchwork quilt context around grids, since her students were currently studying the Colonial period in social studies. Let's enter Liza's class as her children figure out the percentage of colored fabric needed for each patchwork square.

"I counted sixteen in all," Xavier explains to his partner Frederico as they discuss the grid shown in Figure 3.8. "And six are pink."

Frederico agrees and adds, "So it's six sixteenths. But what is that equivalent to?" He goes on to answer his own question. "We could reduce it to three eighths. Oh, look, if you put your hand down the diagonal, it's three out of eight on both sides." Both boys become excited about this, and they draw a line down the diagonal to show Liza (see Figure 3.9).

Liza congratulates them on their nice way to prove the equivalence and then asks, "So what percentage is it?"

After pondering Liza's question, Xavier says, "I know a way to figure out one eighth."

"That's a great start," Liza encourages. "How would you do that?"

"One eighth is half of one fourth, and one fourth is twenty-five percent."

Frederico grins, "Oh, cool. So it's twelve-point-five percent."

"So that's for one eighth," Liza says, supporting their thinking. "What about three eighths?"

"It's three times twelve-point-five—" Frederico ponders a minute and then completes the calculation "—that's thirty-six, thirty-seven, thirty-seven-point-five!"

"So thirty-seven-point-five percent." Xavier completes the process of transforming the fraction three eighths into a percentage.

But Liza pushes further. "How did you know so quickly that one fourth was twenty-five percent?" she asks.

"Because four goes into one hundred twenty-five times. Like four quarters in a dollar," Xavier states matter-of-factly, and Frederico agrees.

"So halving one fourth was a great strategy to get one eighth, because you saw a great relationship and used it. That's super." Then, to challenge them to generalize further, Liza wonders, "What could we do when the

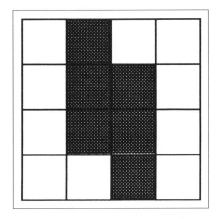

FIGURE 3.8
Patchwork Quilt

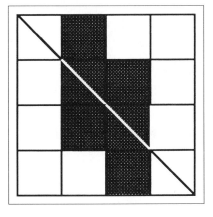

FIGURE 3.9
Xavier and Frederico Added the Diagonal to the Patchwork Quilt

numbers aren't so nice? What if it had been three fifths instead of three eighths?"

The boys are quiet, puzzled for a moment, but then Frederico offers, "We could find one fifth by dividing one hundred by five. That's twenty."

"And then?"

"Times three?" At first he is tentative. But then he continues with certainty, "Yeah, because one fifth is twenty percent. So three fifths is sixty percent. You just divide and multiply."

"And that will always work? Could you guys try to prove that to us in math congress later?"

In this brief vignette we see children being supported as they calculate the percentage of fabric needed. They are encouraged to mathematize the situation, to find ways to see the equivalence of 6/16 to 3/8. They do this by slicing the grid up into various symmetrical portions with their hands. This is what Treffers (1987) has termed "horizontal" mathematizing—mathematizing a context. They are finding ways to interpret their lived world mathematically. However, Liza also encourages them to do "vertical" mathematizing—to generalize relationships, to play in the world of numbers. They are creating a *generalized* procedure that can be used across all equivalence problems, one that can be represented algebraically as $a/b = c/d$, therefore $ad/b = c$!

SUMMING UP . . .

Human beings constructed fractions as a way to represent and deal with fair-sharing situations. The epigraph to this chapter by Heroclitus suggests one such scenario: "Sesostris . . . made a division of the soil of Egypt among the inhabitants. . . . If the river carried away any portion of a man's lot, the king sent persons to examine, and determine by measurement the exact extent of the loss." And R. L. Wilder reminds us, "Mathematics was born and nurtured in a cultural environment. Without the perspective the cultural background affords, a proper appreciation of the content and state of present-day mathematics is hardly possible."

Egyptians made use of doubling and halving, and other than the common fraction 2/3, they relied solely on unit fractions. Babylonians used a number system based on sixty and therefore they constructed sexagesimals. The Chinese used early forms of decimal fractions in connection with their use of the abacus, but it was not until the Renaissance that fractions and decimals as we know them today became commonplace. The Hindu-Arabic base-ten system, as well as ratio problems in the marketplace, brought about the use of common fractions and decimals.

Looking at the time it took these ideas to evolve, we can appreciate the struggle children have as they develop an understanding of ratio and equivalence. The mathematician G. W. Leibniz once said, "Nothing is more important than to see the sources of invention, which are in my opinion more interesting than the inventions themselves." As we observe children like those in Carol, Joel, and Liza's classes inventing these ideas as they grapple with fair sharing, best buys, and fabric percentages, we gain insights into and appreciation for the role of rich contexts in learning and for the cultural climate of the classroom that supports the development of mathematizing.

4 | DEVELOPING BIG IDEAS AND STRATEGIES

All human knowledge thus begins with intuitions, proceeds thence to concepts, and ends with ideas.
—Emmanuel Kant

We have overcome the notion that mathematical truths have an existence independent and apart from our own minds. It is even strange to us that such a notion could ever have existed.
—E. Kasner and J. Newman

You know that I write slowly. This is chiefly because I am never satisfied until I have said as much as possible in a few words, and writing briefly takes far more time than writing at length.
—Karl Friedrich Gauss

In the previous chapters we have witnessed young mathematicians hard at work: dividing submarine sandwiches fairly, proving equivalence, determining best buys. What landmarks are on the landscape of learning? What are some of the critical big ideas that learners construct as they journey toward the horizon of understanding fractions, decimals, and percents? Is there a developmental progression—a progressive schematization—to their strategies? What characterizes the journey?

BIG IDEAS ON THE HORIZON

Part/Whole Relation

James is attempting to make thirds with a strip of paper. He folds it two times, trying to make three equal parts. But making three equal parts with a strip of paper is not as easy as making halves or fourths. Although he tries several times to find the best folds, he eventually makes three equivalent pieces and discards the sliver that is left of the strip. Asked if he thinks he has cut his strip into thirds, he nods affirmatively, demonstrating how he has three equal pieces.

James has succeeded in cutting three equal pieces. They are thirds, but a third of what? They are not thirds of the strip with which he began, because he has snipped a piece off and thrown it away. One of the big ideas at the heart of understanding fractions is that one third is a *part/whole relation*. One third of one strip of paper is not equivalent to one third of another, shorter strip of paper. It is this relational thinking that makes fractions so difficult for children. The parts must be equivalent, but they must also be equivalent in relation to the whole. It is for that reason that Carol Mosesson begins her fraction work with the fair-sharing context described in Chapter 1. Within a context like hers, children do not think of throwing parts away to more easily make congruent pieces. They approach "fractioning" as a relationship, as division, right from the start. But this is only the start of the journey.

Equivalency vs. Congruency

Fractional pieces *do not have to be congruent, only equivalent.* By starting with fair sharing, Carol allows her students to explore this big idea as well. Throughout the investigation, these children are immersed in proving equivalent relationships. Although some children cut the subs into unit fractions to share them (three subs for four kids = $\frac{1}{2} + \frac{1}{4}$), others cut each sub into four pieces ($3 \times \frac{1}{4}$). As children cut and move pieces of the subs to prove where to make a fair cut, they are exploring how the quantity stays the same, even though the pieces look different. Compensation is involved: what you gain in one place you must lose in another.

Connecting Multiplication and Division to Fractions

By starting with a fair-sharing context, Carol allows her children to explore a third big idea, the *connection of multiplication and division to fractions*. In this context they are exploring both partitive and quotative division. (Readers not familiar with these terms should see volume 2 of this series.) Three subs shared among four kids (three divided, or *partitioned,* out to four) results in three out of four parts of one sub (*quotative division*). Along with proving equivalence, students are investigating—and constructing—the idea that one fourth of each sub times three equals three fourths of one sub.

When fractions are introduced right from the start within fair-sharing contexts, as division, a misconception often seen in traditional classrooms is usually avoided. In traditional classrooms, fractions are often introduced as a number within a measurement (or quotative) model. For example, pizzas or similar whole entities are shown with various-size shaded parts, and children are asked to identify the amount of the shaded part. When fractions are treated as numbers in the beginning of the journey—too early on—learners often assume that the greater the denominator the greater the amount— $\frac{1}{8} > \frac{1}{7}$ because 8 > 7. Even when they begin to understand that the denominator is a divisor, and therefore the greater the number of pieces, the smaller the amount, the relationship of the numerator to the denominator escapes them.

Jessica is a case in point. She is trying to prove that ⅔ is greater than ⅝. Her answer is correct, but her logic is hard to follow. She writes, "I think ⅔ is bigger because it is a smaller number than ⅝. In fractions the biggest one is smallest like 1/16 is smaller than ⅔." She seems to understand that the *bigger the denominator the smaller the amount*. Her example of 1/16 fits this explanation. But what does she mean by "⅔ is bigger because it is a smaller number"? Does she understand that when comparing two fractions the numerator also matters and, more to the point, that *if the denominators are common only the numerators matter*? And reciprocally, *if the numerators are common only the denominators matter*? How would she compare ⅞ to ⅔? To understand the relationship of the numerator and denominator, one must understand the relationship of multiplication and division.

Meg demonstrates that she has passed this landmark when she explains in her math journal "5 bars divided by 6 kids is 5 × ⅙. The ⅚ mark on the strip [fraction bar] is also 5 × ⅙. The multiplication and the division are related. Fractions are multiplication *and* division!"

The Whole Matters: Making Things Equivalent

Tanya, on the other hand, understands that both the numerator and denominator matter, but she has not worked out a way to compare them. She writes, "⅝ has more parts. ⅔ has much more bigger slices than ⅝ but ⅝ has much smaller slices." She draws a picture of two bars to represent her thinking (see Figure 4.1), but the two bars are not the same size, and she concludes that ⅝ is more. What appears to be holding her back is the big idea that in order *to compare two fractions, the whole must be the same*—⅔ of 12 is less than ⅝ of 16. Walter and Steve (see Figures 4.2 and 4.3) are further along on the landscape. They have found several ways to prove their thinking about which is larger, ⅔ or ⅝.

This big idea—*the whole matters because fractions are relations*—will appear again and again in the landscape. It is critical to understanding and proving equivalence, but it also is critical as children explore operations. Because children often add numerators and then denominators (transferring procedures that worked with whole numbers), Toni Cameron and Shari Levy wanted to hit this misconception head on. They asked their students

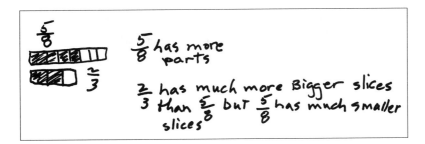

FIGURE 4.1   *Tanya's Strategy*

to prove that ½ + ⅔ did not equal ⅖. This instructional decision was a good one. As children worked to prove that ½ + ⅔ did not equal ⅖, their thinking about fractions deepened. Joe writes, "I'll make 100 the whole. ⅓ of 100 is 33⅓; ½ of 100 is 50; so that's 83⅓; ⅖ of 100 is only 40." This strategy already shows an understanding of the need to use the same whole. But Joe's thinking becomes quite elegant: "½ is bigger than ⅖ itself." And later: "⅖ = 40 [of 100] and that is ⅕ + ⅕, and ⅕ is less than ⅓ and less than ½." Joe has passed the landmark of treating the fraction relationally. He knows that the whole matters.

Alice and Joanie exhibit the same ability to make the wholes the same as they compare and find the difference between ³⁄₁₀ and ⅖. Alice uses several models: percentages, decimals, bar, pie, and number line (see Figure 4.4). In each the wholes are equivalent. Joanie makes common denominators (see Figure 4.5).

Relations on Relations

When comparing, adding, and subtracting fractions and making equivalent fractions, there is only one whole to consider, and both fractions must be treated in relation to it. But as children begin to explore the operations of

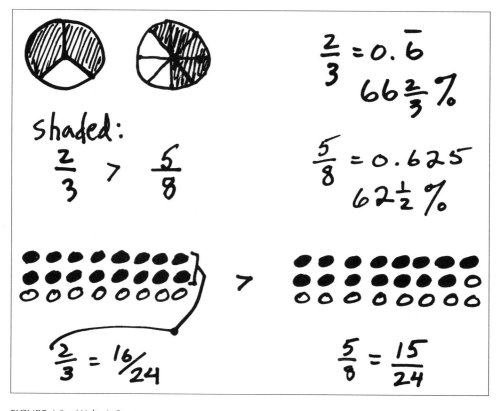

FIGURE 4.2 *Walter's Strategy*

multiplication and division with fractions, there are two wholes to consider: there are *relations on relations*. For example, Nora figures out a way to share five candy bars fairly with six children (see Figure 4.6). She cuts each of the first three bars in half and the fourth bar into quarters, reminiscent of Egyptian unit fractions. When she cuts the last bar, however, she is faced with what to call the sixths of the half. The half is now the whole, which is why we say ⅙ of it. But there are *two* wholes to consider: the candy bar is one whole, half the candy bar is another whole. The sliver is ⅙ of the half, but it is 1/12 of the whole candy bar. Nora concludes (erroneously) that it is ⅓. She halves the denominator instead of doubling it.

The situation is the same when dividing fractions. There are two wholes, because the situation involves relations on relations. Let's listen in on a conversation two inservice teachers, Jamie and Diane, are having as they try to figure out how many quarter-inches fit into two thirds of an inch. They begin by drawing a line to represent an inch, and they mark it into thirds in order to represent the two thirds of an inch.

"This is our starting point," Jamie announces.

On the bottom of their paper Diane draws a line the same length and demarcates it into fourths. "Okay, so here is the same inch marked into fourths.

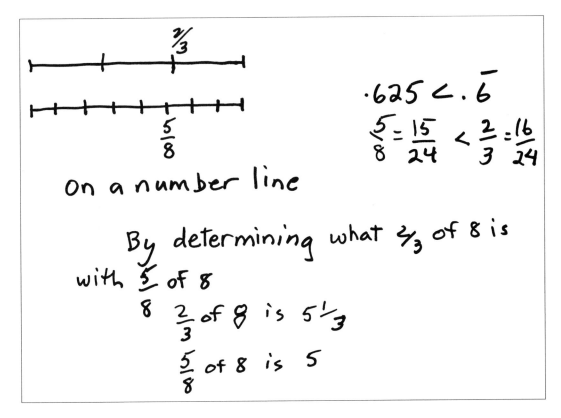

FIGURE 4.3   *Steve's Strategy*

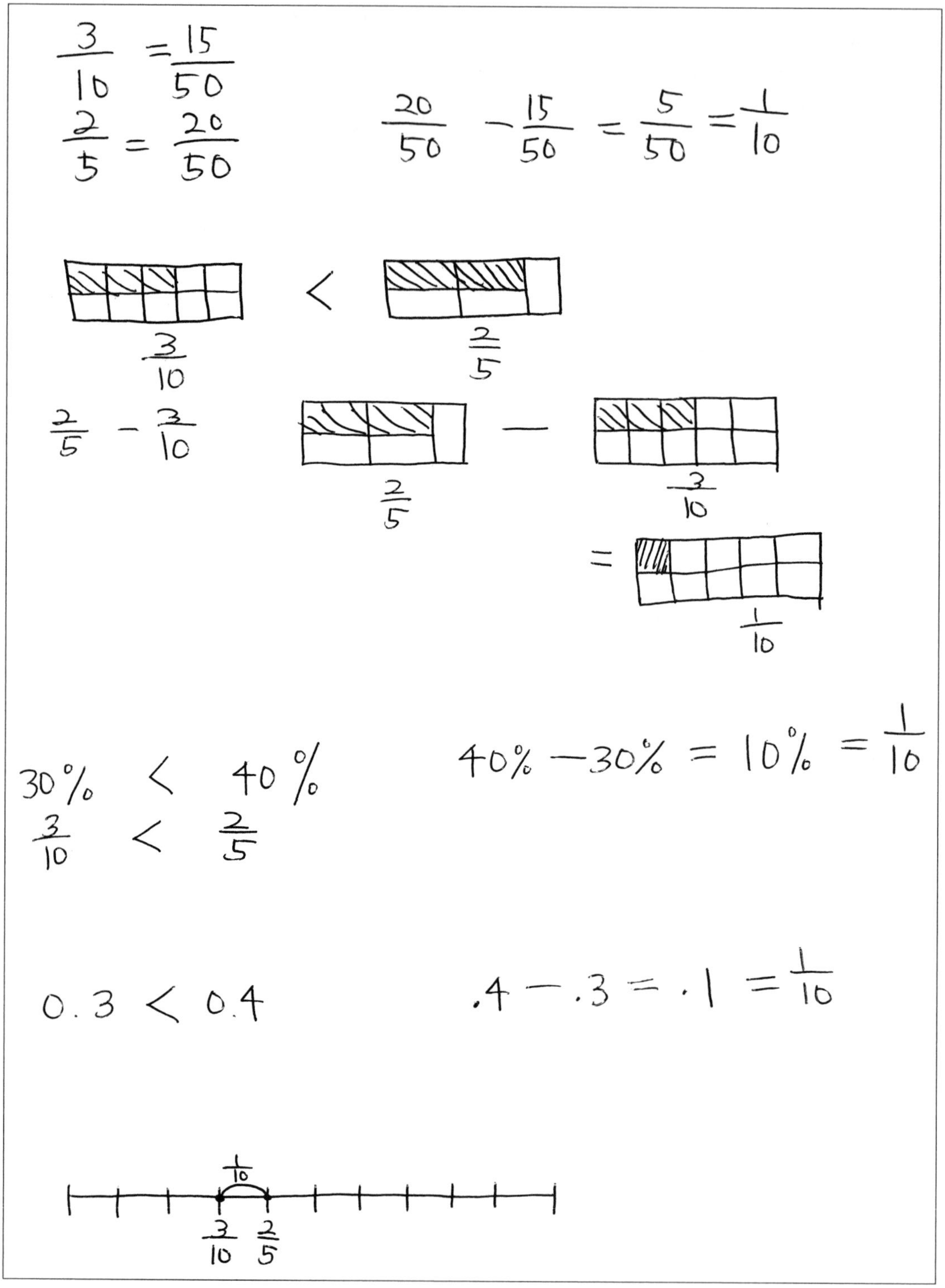

$$\frac{3}{10} = \frac{15}{50}$$

$$\frac{2}{5} = \frac{20}{50}$$

$$\frac{20}{50} - \frac{15}{50} = \frac{5}{50} = \frac{1}{10}$$

$$\frac{3}{10} < \frac{2}{5}$$

$$\frac{2}{5} - \frac{3}{10}$$

$$\frac{2}{5} - \frac{3}{10} = \frac{1}{10}$$

$$30\% < 40\%$$

$$\frac{3}{10} < \frac{2}{5}$$

$$40\% - 30\% = 10\% = \frac{1}{10}$$

$$0.3 < 0.4$$

$$.4 - .3 = .1 = \frac{1}{10}$$

FIGURE 4.4   *Alice's Strategy*

Step two!" She pauses, laughs, and says with a quizzical look, "Now what do we do?"

"Well, the fourth of an inch fits in two thirds of an inch between two and three times," Jamie quickly responds.

"I know, but how much more than two times? That's what I don't know!"

"What if we make the fractions equivalent?" Jamie suggests.

"Okay, so what shall we use, twelfths?" Without waiting for Jamie's response, Diane proceeds to add $\frac{4}{12}$ and $\frac{8}{12}$ to the top line, equivalent to the thirds.

"Let's make a new line for both the thirds and the fourths," Jamie suggests. Diane agrees and they draw a third line in between the other two. On

$$\frac{2}{5} = \frac{4}{10} \qquad \frac{2}{5} = \frac{8}{20} \qquad \frac{2}{5} = \frac{12}{30}$$

$$\frac{4}{10} - \frac{3}{10} = \frac{1}{10} \qquad \frac{3}{10} = \frac{6}{20} \qquad \frac{3}{10} = \frac{9}{30}$$

$$\frac{8}{20} - \frac{6}{20} = \frac{2}{20} \qquad \frac{12}{30} - \frac{9}{30} = \frac{3}{30}$$

$$\frac{2}{5} = \frac{16}{40} \qquad \frac{2}{5} = \frac{20}{50} \qquad \frac{2}{5} = \frac{24}{60}$$

$$\frac{3}{10} = \frac{12}{40} \qquad \frac{3}{10} = \frac{15}{50} \qquad \frac{3}{10} = \frac{18}{60}$$

$$\frac{16}{40} - \frac{12}{40} = \frac{4}{40} \qquad \frac{20}{50} - \frac{15}{50} = \frac{5}{50} \qquad \frac{24}{60} - \frac{18}{60} = \frac{6}{60}$$

FIGURE 4.5   *Joanie's Strategy*

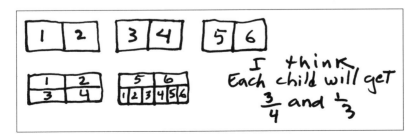

FIGURE 4.6   *Nora's Strategy*

this they mark the fourths with twelfths—$\frac{3}{12}$, $\frac{6}{12}$, and $\frac{9}{12}$. On the top they draw the two quarter-inches, ending at the $\frac{6}{12}$ mark. "Okay, so it goes this far," Jamie continues drawing a line from the $\frac{6}{12}$ above. "Two twelfths more," she concludes with a flourish, then reduces to $\frac{1}{6}$, "two and one sixth." (Their work thus far is shown in Figure 4.7.)

Diane looks puzzled.

"Want me to explain it again?" Jamie offers.

"No. I get what you said. But two and one sixth what? This one sixth is one sixth of the inch. The two refers to the two quarter-inches. My head hurts. I keep losing the question we are trying to figure out." Diane is grappling with the fact that there are two wholes and they need to be worked with simultaneously. The quarter-inch is a whole, but so is the inch! The question is how many *quarter-inches* fit? The answer must be in relation to the quarter-inch. As Diane ponders the situation, she begins to make sense out of it. "The third quarter of an inch would go to the nine-twelfths mark. So these marks are for seven twelfths and eight twelfths. I think maybe they are thirds of the quarter-inch."

Jamie is now pondering the situation too, and she begins to realize the original problem in her thinking. "You're right, so this mark is one sixth of an inch, but it's two thirds of a quarter-inch. Wow, this is hard. No wonder my kids have a hard time with division of fractions! It's like the whole keeps switching."

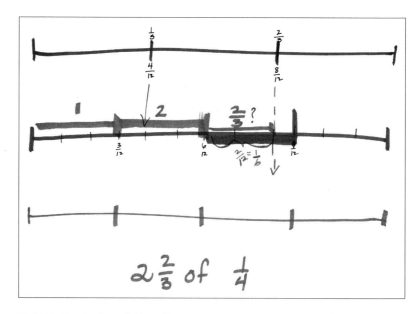

FIGURE 4.7 *Jamie and Diane Figuring Out How Many Quarter-Inches Fit into Two Thirds of an Inch*

Jamie and Diane are having a difficult time for exactly the reason Jamie states, "the whole keeps switching." There are two wholes, and the problem requires thinking about a relation on a relation.

Decimals and Percentage Equivalents

Decimals and percents are really just specific equivalents of fractional relations. Decimals are fractional base-ten equivalents making use of place value, and percents are relationships based on a one-hundred-part whole. Many of the big ideas are the same as those pertaining to fractions.

The children in Paul Maasen's fifth-grade classroom, in the Netherlands, are exploring percentages. Let's listen in as they grapple, once again, with the idea that the whole matters. Paul is telling his students about two advertisements he saw in a newspaper. Both are for department store sales. The first store, Van Merckesteijn's, advertises 25 percent off; the second, Doek's, advertises 40 percent off. "If you wanted to buy something, which store would go to? Van Merckesteijn's or Doek's?" Paul asks.

All children are adamant—Doek's gives you the best buy. Paul does not ask for any arguments at first. Instead, he gives them the opportunity to discuss in groups why they think shopping at Doek's is better.

Four boys—Anton, Chuck, James, and Edward—talk among themselves, often building on to what has just been said.

"Because then you only have sixty percent left to pay," Anton says.

"Forty precent is cheaper," James adds.

Chuck and Anton now discuss what reduction means: if you get a 40 percent reduction, you have to pay 60 percent of the price. All four boys are aware of that.

Chuck: "Forty, yes, forty percent, then you get to subtract more."

Anton: "Yes, but I have a hundred minus twenty-five—then I have seventy-five left. And if you take forty away from a hundred, you have only sixty left. Doek's is cheaper."

Chuck: "Yes, but you cannot use forty. For instance, say the price is a hundred guilders. You don't add forty percent. You subtract forty percent. So Doek's is cheaper."

Anton: "Yes, but twenty-five percent is one fourth of a hundred, and forty percent is almost one half of a hundred."

Chuck: "Yes, just about. But at Van Merckesteijn's you have to pay one fourth, and then you—"

Anton: "No, you get one fourth off, and at Doek's you get nearly one half off."

Paul is using this reduction context to have his students discuss what these advertisements really tell them. He knows students at first usually only pay attention to the amount of reduction. However, reduction in percentage gives a relative measure, not an absolute measure. First, the original price of an item might not be the same at both stores. Second, the percentage in the context is an operator—it is forty one-hundredths *of* the price. For example, if we can buy the same trousers at 40 percent off a 150-guilder price tag or 25 percent off a 100-guilder price tag, the latter pair is much cheaper. Paul wants his students to explore the idea that the whole matters.

These four students are clearly struggling with this idea. James continues, "You buy some clothes for fifty guilders and then at Van Merckesteijn's it would be—then it might be forty—forty guilders. And at Van Merckesteijn's, he might have—half—yes, because forty percent is a big discount." James is clearly confused.

Chuck makes another attempt. "For instance, there are pants, costing—very expensive pants—new ones. They cost two hundred guilders because they are made of very special—because it is made of very special material that has just been invented. And you get a twenty-five percent discount. Then you'd have—you'd have about—"

The four boys are still struggling. They are treating the percentage reduction as a quantity rather than as a relation and struggling over how to take 40 percent of an amount.

In another part of the room, Paul is listening to six other students as they heatedly discuss the issue. They begin talking about the price of the products they buy, and soon the conversation turns to how the two stores might have different original prices. "Oh yes, that would be possible, wouldn't it? Is it important to know?" Paul asks.

"Yes," the students say.

Alan immediately gives an example. "Maybe you'd buy something that costs a lot more. Maybe they've got a sixty-guilder sweater, on which you'll get a forty percent discount. And now the same sweater at another store costs, let's say, forty guilders and you get twenty-five percent off."

Anja picks up on his thinking. "Well, in both shops you don't have to have the same price. For instance, Doek's can give the best discount, but maybe they are the most expensive. A sweater might cost sixty guilders there, and at Merckesteijn's only twenty-five guilders."

Paul paraphrases, "So you are saying, if one shop has a price of sixty guilders and the other has a price of twenty-five guilders, it is important to know?"

David goes back to the context. "Two shops advertise to get customers. They try to follow the laws of economics. They want to sell their goods. If one charges sixty guilders and the other twenty-five—only that doesn't happen in any real shop, because everyone would always go [to the cheaper store even] when there wasn't any sale on. Your example is impossible. It's much too much. Then you would be right. But if the price is the same, then Doek's is always cheaper." Edo clarifies for the group, "If both sweaters cost sixty guilders originally, then I would go to Doek's, because it offers a bigger discount percentage. But if the price is different originally, it matters. It is important to know what the price is that is discounted. You cannot just say forty percent is a better discount than twenty-five percent, because you have to know what price the discount is on."

With decimals and percents, just as with fractions, the whole matters. Forty percent means $^{40}/_{100}$. The whole is 100. But when describing a discount, tip, or interest rate, we are talking about 40 percent of another amount. The operation of multiplication is involved. It is 40 percent of, say, sixty guilders, or $.40 \times 60$. This is a big idea for children—one that we saw children struggling with earlier as they explored fractions.

Place Value

Although many of the big ideas about fractions also underlie decimals and percents, the place value aspect is new. We learned in Chapter 3 that the Hindu-Arabic system was around for several hundred years, and decimals had still not been invented. Pierre-Simon de Laplace wrote, "It is India that gave us the ingenious method of expressing all numbers by means of ten symbols, each symbol receiving a value of position as well as an absolute value; a profound and important idea which appears so simple to us now that we ignore its true merit. But its very simplicity and the great ease which it has lent to computations put our arithmetic in the first rank of useful inventions; and we shall appreciate the grandeur of the achievement the more when we remember that it escaped the genius of Archimedes and Apollonius, two of the greatest men produced by antiquity" (cited in Eves 1988). Even though children may have an understanding of place value as it relates to whole numbers, extending this idea to a decimal system is an important horizon with many landmarks along the way.

Carol Mosesson decided to immerse her students in an investigation with the calculator as a way of exploring this horizon. She asked them to investigate what the calculator does when fractions are entered into the calculator as division, for example when $^{3}/_{5}$ is entered as $3 \div 5$. Children began exploring a list of various fractions—$^{3}/_{5}$, $^{3}/_{6}$, $^{4}/_{8}$, $^{6}/_{10}$, $^{8}/_{10}$, $^{8}/_{100}$, $^{54}/_{10}$, $^{1}/_{1000}$, etc.— and they added to this list as they went along. Recording while they worked, they made a table of their results, noticing several patterns and exploring why they were happening. Here, in their own words, are a few of the big ideas they constructed:

1. "Fractions with denominators of 10 have the numerator in the answer. We noticed that whatever fraction we did, the answer was there already. As long as 10 was the denominator. We think the calculator is just making tenths. For example $^{3}/_{10}$ was .3, $^{6}/_{10}$ was .6, $^{32}/_{10}$ was 3.2, etc. We tried bunches more, and the same thing kept happening. Once we realized this we knew that if we reduced a fraction to one where the denominator was 10, we would already know the decimal. For example: $^{35}/_{50} = ^{7}/_{10} = .7$."
2. "All fractions that are equivalent to $^{1}/_{2}$ are equal to .5. That's just because .5 is $^{5}/_{10}$, and that is a half, too."
3. "If you keep adding a 0 to the divisor, the decimal keeps moving over a place. For example, 1234 divided by 10 = 123.4; divided by 100 =

12.34; divided by 1000 = 1.234; divided by 10000 = .1234; divided by 100000 = .01234. It just keeps bumping over just like when you have whole numbers and you multiply or divide by 10 or 100, etc."

4. "If you look at the number you are dividing by, the decimal quotient will have the same number of digits to the right of the decimal point as the number of zeroes in the divisor. For example, $\frac{1}{10}$ = .1; $\frac{1}{100}$ = .01; $\frac{1}{1000}$ = .001. This is so awesome. You just have to count the number of zeroes. It happens because that is the number of times you are dividing by ten."

It is this last big idea that gets to the heart of the place value involved. It is this idea that will bring children to realize that calculation with decimals can be done just as with whole numbers—albeit with division or multiplication by ten at the end.

STRATEGIES ON THE HORIZON

Big ideas are critical in developing understanding, but ultimately it is the mathematizing of contexts that matters. The development of strategies that children exhibit as they come to understand what it means to make things equivalent is an important component of this mathematizing. How does one make common denominators, for example? How does one establish equivalent fractions? What are the different strategies children construct as they attempt to do so?

Dawn Selnes and Toni Cameron tell a class of fifth graders about Toni's recent trip to Holland and about how she discovered the large flat pancakes called *pannenkoeken*. These are about as large as a medium pizza and flat, somewhat like a large crepe. One is often too large for one person to eat alone, and so they are shared. Toni wonders: if they make them in class and invite guests, and if they want everyone to have three fourths of a pancake, how many people can be in the group in relation to the number of pancakes?

Teddy and Reggie use *repeated addition*. Teddy tries to add ¾ several times but struggles. Finally he adds one pancake and two children each time and produces the erroneous table in Figure 4.8a. Although he knows that repeated addition is a way to mathematize the situation, he has not yet developed a strategy for adding these fractions or for keeping the ratio constant. Reggie's work (see Figure 4.8b) is similar. He writes about the need for repeated addition of ¾ but must draw pictures to do the repeated addition.

Laura, Tiffany, and Lara begin to double. Laura (see Figure 4.9a) knows doubling is a strategy that will keep the ratio equivalent; her prose describes the needed relation. However, she continues throughout to confuse what is being doubled, children or pancakes, and thus her answers are not equivalent. Lara (see Figure 4.9b) and Tiffany (see Figure 4.9c) are nearby on the landscape, but they are able to double consistently. Tiffany even writes, "What you have to do is just double and the doubling goes on forever." Because their strategy is *doubling*, however, they miss many of the possibilities, and they have not yet worked out a generalized way to establish an equivalent ratio other than the specific case of doubling. Nevertheless, this is a beginning step toward keeping the ratio equivalent.

Vicki's, Ned's, and Daniel's strategy is to use multiples. Vicki writes, "The number of pancakes have to be a multiple of 3. The number of children have to be a multiple of 4." Daniel's work is similar. He *keeps the ratio constant* (3 to 4) in the same way and writes, "It keeps going forever." Ned's words are a bit more elegant but the strategy is the same: "The number of

$$\frac{3}{4} + \frac{3}{4} + \frac{3}{4} \quad \text{2 pancakes and 3 children}$$
①   ②   ③

$$\frac{3}{4} + \frac{3}{4} + \frac{3}{4} + \frac{3}{4} + \frac{3}{4} = \quad \text{3 pancakes and 5 children}$$
① ② ③ ④ ⑤

4 pancakes and 7 children
5 pancakes and 9 children
6 pancakes and 11 children
7 pancakes and 13 children

and you can keep going

FIGURE 4.8a
Teddy's Strategy

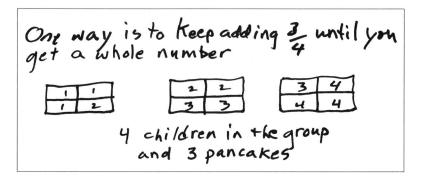

One way is to keep adding $\frac{3}{4}$ until you get a whole number

1	1
1	2

2	2
3	3

3	4
4	4

4 children in the group
and 3 pancakes

FIGURE 4.8b *Reggie's Strategy*

pancakes increases by 3, every 4 children." By using this 3 to 4 ratio they are able to produce more possibilities than were produced with the doubling strategy, but they, too, still miss many.

Maria efficiently uses a *ratio table*. Since one child gets three fourth of a pancake, and four children get three, five children get three and three fourths.

Tom and Elsa have found a way to generalize (see Figure 4.10). They *treat the ratio, ¾, as an operator.* Elsa even writes, "¾x, x = the number of people." This strategy allows figuring out how many pancakes (fractional amounts)

Four children and 3 pancakes
6 children and 8 because
double the pancakes and get 6
and double the children and get 8

16 children and 12 pancakss
24 children and 32 pancakes
64 children and 48 pancakes
96 children and 128 pancakes

FIGURE 4.9a   *Laura's Strategy*

$$\frac{3}{4} \times 4 \qquad \begin{array}{l}\text{4 children}\\ \text{3 pancakes}\end{array}$$

4 children	3 pancakes
8 children	6 pancakes
8 + 8 = 16 children	12 pancakes = 6+6
16 + 16 = 32 children	24 pancakes = 12+12

FIGURE 4.9b   *Lara's Strategy*

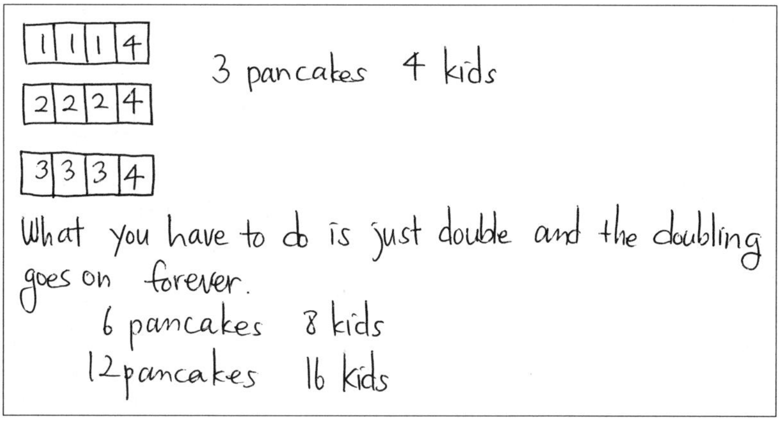

| 1 | 1 | 1 | 4 |

3 pancakes   4 kids

| 2 | 2 | 2 | 4 |

| 3 | 3 | 3 | 4 |

What you have to do is just double and the doubling
goes on forever.
        6 pancakes   8 kids
      12 pancakes   16 kids

FIGURE 4.9c   *Tiffany's Strategy*

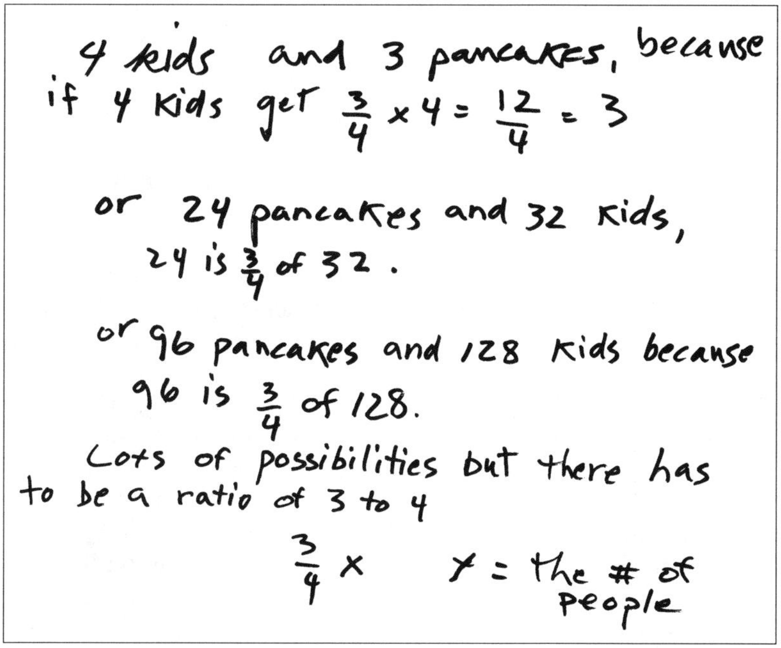

4 kids and 3 pancakes, because
if 4 kids get $\frac{3}{4} \times 4 = \frac{12}{4} = 3$

or 24 pancakes and 32 kids,
24 is $\frac{3}{4}$ of 32.

or 96 pancakes and 128 kids because
96 is $\frac{3}{4}$ of 128.
Lots of possibilities but there has
to be a ratio of 3 to 4

$\frac{3}{4} \times$ $x =$ the # of
                              people

FIGURE 4.10   *Tom and Elsa's Strategy*

are needed for any group of people, e.g. 3¾ pancakes for 5 people. This strategy is generalized even further when one realizes that *cross-multiplying* keeps the ratio constant, i.e., $a/b = c/d$; $ad = bc$.

The strategies these students have developed, although they are not comprehensive, may be helpful to teachers as they observe and reflect on their own students' strategies and ideas. There are many others on the landscape as well.

SUMMING UP . . .

Each of the epigraphs at the beginning of this chapter reflects a different aspect of learning. When the philosopher Emmanual Kant wrote, "All human knowledge thus begins with intuitions, proceeds thence to concepts, and ends with ideas" (cited in Hilbert 1962) he was describing the importance of critical, overarching "big ideas" in the development of thought. When children are grappling to understand fractions, several important big ideas often puzzle them—ideas that are developmental leaps, that sometimes require a shift in perspective. For example, children often struggle with the fact that fractions depict part/whole relation and that the parts do not need to be congruent, only equivalent. They need to construct the idea that the whole matters and that fractions are connected to multiplication and division. Decimals and percents are specific instances of these ideas, but they bring up new insights about place value.

Historically we developed a sequence of instructional objectives by analyzing the discipline of mathematics. For fractions, decimals, and percents, for example, educators and curriculum developers designed activities that they thought progressed from simple to complex. We began with shaded parts of a whole and ended with the division of fractions. But now, as E. Kasner and J. Newman (1940) express so aptly, "We have overcome the notion that mathematical truths have an existence independent and apart from our own minds. It is even strange to us that such a notion could ever have existed." It is the development of ideas, in history and in each individual child, that should give us clues to a sequence—clues to the landscape, the landmarks, and the emerging horizons.

For children to become able to mathematize their world, they need to be allowed to do so in their own meaning-making ways as they are learning. They need to grapple with big ideas and progressively refine their strategies. They may use repeated addition, doubling, multiples, the ratio table, or ratios as operators. Their strategies will not always be efficient, or even sufficient, given where they are at that moment on the journey. But there is a developmental progression to their strategies. Karl Friedrich Gauss said, "You know that I write slowly. This is chiefly because I am never satisfied until I have said as much as possible in a few words, and writing briefly takes far more time than writing at length" (cited in Simmons 1992). Part of what it means to do mathematics is to explore relationships and find ways to make your procedures, proofs, and strategies elegant. Children's mathematical development exemplifies this, and when we support their progressive development—rather than trying to get them all to the same objective or procedure in the same amount of time—we support the human drive to create, to know, and to make efficient. This drive for understanding, efficiency, and elegance is at the heart of what it means to be a young mathematician at work.

5 | DEVELOPING MATHEMATICAL MODELS

The essential fact is that all the pictures that science now draws of nature, and which alone seem capable of according with observational facts, are mathematical pictures.

—Sir James Jeans

The purpose of models is not to fit the data but to sharpen the questions.

—Samuel Karlin

WHAT ARE MATHEMATICAL MODELS?

When mathematics is understood to be mathematizing—the human activity of organizing and interpreting reality mathematically—rather than a closed system of content to be transmitted or even discovered, mathematical models become very important. It is impossible to discuss mathematizing without simultaneously discussing models.

Models are representations of relationships that mathematicians have constructed over time as they have reflected on how one thing can be changed into another and as they have generalized ideas, strategies, and representations across contexts. Although models are used as a lens when new mathematical questions are being explored, they are themselves constructed in the development of our mathematical awareness.

In a sense, models are mental maps mathematicians use as they organize their activity, solve problems, or explore relationships. For example, when mathematicians are thinking about number, they may have a number line in mind. They think about where numbers are in relation to one another on this line, and they imagine moving back and forth along it. A geometric model of number is another helpful mental map. For example, one might imagine 64 transformed into a square (8×8) and then into a cube ($4 \times 4 \times 4$), and 27 as a smaller cube ($3 \times 3 \times 3$), and then examine how these numbers are related to each other. Some models depict a network of number relationships based on benchmark numbers, their neighbors, and their use in operations. For example, a mathematician might see the number 64 and immediately think of 2 to the 6th power, or $70 - 6$, or 32 doubled, or 8^2, or $^{128}\!/_2$, or $100 - 36 = 10^2 - 6^2$. Or, to use a fraction example, one might think of $\frac{8}{10}$ as .8, or 80%, or $\frac{4}{5}$, or 2 to the third power divided by 10 to the first power, or 8 submarine sandwiches shared among 10 people, or $8 \times \frac{1}{10}$, or 8 out of 10 parts. Four fifths can be a number; it can be an operator. One might also think about it as $1 - \frac{1}{5}$, or $1 - .2$. Other models depict growth patterns—a Cartesian linear plotting of (.8,1), (4,5), (8,10), (12,15), etc., for example.

MODELING ACTIONS AND SITUATIONS

When a young child attempts to make lines on paper to indicate the tree on her street, she begins to model her world. The tree, as she has experienced it, is three-dimensional. She has walked around it, touched the bark, felt the shade from the leaves overhead. The lines she makes on paper are a *representation of* the tree on a two-dimensional plane to communicate to others what she knows a tree to be. The representation is not a copy of what she *sees*; it is a construction, within a medium, of what she *knows*. It is a creation.

Children's early models are usually representations of their actions within the situation. For example, when Dawn Selnes asked her students how much chocolate each of six children would get if she shared five bars among them evenly, Joanie, like many of her classmates, models the distribution process on paper (see Figure 5.1). She draws the passing out of the bars. First she cuts the top two bars into thirds so that each child gets one third of a bar. Then she repeats this action with the next two bars. Since she is left with only one bar, and she wants it to be fair, she cuts this bar into six pieces. Thus she arrives at an answer of $\frac{2}{3} + \frac{1}{6}$. Rebecca and Vicki's strategies, though different from Joanie's, also very closely model the situation. Rebecca (Figure 5.2a) even adds names to the children and the pieces! Vicki (Figure 5.2b) models the distribution with numerals.

As Joanie, Rebecca, and Vicki and their classmates participate in activities like these, as they are encouraged and supported in mathematizing situations, their models will go beyond representations of their actions and move toward more generalized models of strategies. They will move from models *of* thinking to models *for* thinking (Gravemeijer 1999, 2000). According to Gravemeijer (2000, 9), "The shift from *model of* to *model for* concurs with a shift in the students' thinking, from thinking about the modeled context situation, to a focus on mathematical relations." This is a major landmark in mathematical development.

FACILITATING THE DEVELOPMENT OF MODELING: THE ROLE OF CONTEXT

In previous chapters we have witnessed how teachers made use of context to support the development of their students' mathematizing. Varying the context from distributing submarine sandwiches fairly to searching for the best buy in cat food brings up several ideas, models, and landmarks—the relationship of fractions to division and multiplication, and the use of the ratio table, for example. How does context affect children's mathematizing, and how can teachers use it to support the development of mathematical modeling? What models are important regarding fractions, and how do we help children generalize across situations—go beyond the modeling *of* a specific situation to interpreting a situation *with* a powerful mathematical model as a tool *for* thinking? To explore these questions, we invite you to observe Randy, Meg, and Jennie as they explore several different situations.

Partitive and Quotative Models

Jake Robinson introduces a new context for his class to investigate. "Over the next few weeks we will be doing a lot of cooking in class, and I don't want to go out and buy a lot of measuring cups. So I thought we might make our own." He holds up several cylindrical glasses. "I made paper strips that are as long as these glasses are high. Let's mark the paper strips carefully, one for halves, one for thirds, one for fourths, one for fifths, etc. These strips can then be glued on the glasses and we'll have our own measuring cups."

FIGURE 5.1 *Joanie's Strategy*

Randy, Meg, and Jennie take the strips Jake has provided and immediately set to work. "Halves are easy," Randy states as he folds a strip down the middle, making two equal parts.

"And we could just do that again to make fourths." Meg takes another strip and demonstrates how she can make fourths by folding the halves in half again.

"Oh, yeah. And we can keep doing that—what does that make?" At first Randy is not sure as he folds the fourths in half, but then he says, "Oh. Eighths. Cool. A half of a fourth is an eighth." With pencils they begin to mark their strips.

Jennie has decided to take another tack. She has gotten a ruler to measure the strips and comments, "The strips are six inches long—so the halfway point is three." She makes a mark on the strip as she measures and then draws a line and writes ½. "So now I'll do quarters—what's one quarter of six?" Randy and Meg, who are busy marking their strips, don't respond. Jennie tries two. "No, that's two plus two plus two plus two, that's eight—so it's too big."

FIGURE 5.2a *Rebecca's Strategy*

Randy becomes aware of her struggle and suggests, "Two could be thirds, because three times two is six." Jennie agrees with him and makes lines at two inches and four inches, labeling them ⅓ and ⅔. "But how do I do fourths," she asks, still puzzled.

"It's easy," Meg declares. "Just fold the half in half, like we did." She demonstrates with her folded strip.

Jennie still struggles with the ruler, not wanting to fold her paper. Finally she succeeds. "Oh, I know—it's one-and-a-half inches. That fits four times!"

Randy and Meg are now struggling with the folding of thirds and sixths. Folding paper strips into thirds is difficult, and (as we discussed in Chapter 4) children often will snip a little piece off to get the three equal pieces, unwittingly changing the whole. Randy does just that. He grabs a pair of scissors and carefully snips a very thin piece off the end. "There," he says, satisfied. "And now sixths are easy because it's half of this third."

"And if we do a third of that piece, I think we get the ninths." Meg declares. "See." She counts three for each third, pointing to each with three fingers. "Three, six, nine!"

Jennie easily completes the sixths, because each sixth is one inch. For twelfths she marks half inches, commenting to Randy and Meg, "Now I'm using your strategy. It's half of a sixth—so the twelfths are one-half inches!"

"That's too big, I think," Randy says as he lines up his twelfths with hers. "See I did the twelfths, too! I took one half of my sixths. And my pieces are really little." Randy is about to meet with disequilibrium—just as he nears what he thinks is completion! In his mind, his markings have been correct. Where did he go wrong?

Randy's model is one of equal parts. He thinks, *If I have three equal parts, they are thirds. One third is one out of three equal parts.* He also treats fractions here as *operators.* He takes ½ *of* ⅓. He operates on the ⅓ with the ½. Of course ½ of ⅓ of something less than a whole strip is not the same as ½ of ⅓ of the whole strip. He still has to grapple with this big idea.

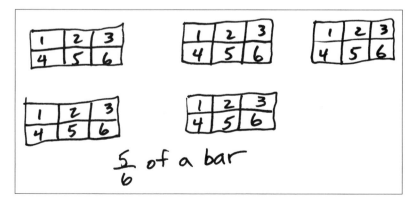

FIGURE 5.2b   *Vicki's Strategy*

Let's return to the issue of modeling and the role of context. In the first scenario (the candy bars), the problem was modeled by all three children as *distributive* (*partitive*) division: a *ratio* of candy bars to children. The fair-sharing situation helped them realize that no part could, or should, be thrown away. It also helped develop the idea of fractions as division and their subsequent relationship to multiplication: five candy bars shared by six children equals $5 \times \frac{1}{6}$, or $\frac{5}{6}$ of a bar each.

Division can also be thought of as *measurement* (*quotative*). How many bags of cookies can I make if I have twelve cookies and I put three in a bag? How many times does three fit? Three *goes into* twelve four times. Or, as Jennie says in the fraction context as she measures, "One-and-a-half inches fits four times," so it's one fourth of the six-inch strip.

Traditionally, teachers started fraction work with quotative contexts. In the early grades children were often asked to shade in parts of a whole and label them with the appropriate fraction. For example, two triangles shaded in a regular hexagon (see Figure 5.3) would be labeled $\frac{2}{6}$, or six slices of pizza out of eight would be labeled $\frac{6}{8}$. As we moved up the grades, we often brought out Cuisennaire rods or fraction bars to teach equivalence. A quotative model is important, but it is not the place to start on the landscape, because doing so often results in the misconception that Randy has encountered—that one third is one of three equal parts. The relationship with the whole gets missed.

Partitive and quotative division models also surface when one thinks about division with fractions—$\frac{2}{3}$ divided by $\frac{1}{2}$, for example. Each kind of model will likely bring up different ideas. To understand why, draw a picture to help you solve these two problems:

I used $\frac{2}{3}$ of a can of paint to cover $\frac{1}{2}$ the floor of the porch. How much paint will be needed for the whole floor?

John is baking a cake and only has a $\frac{1}{2}$-cup measuring tool. The recipe calls for $\frac{2}{3}$ of a cup of flour. How many times should he fill his $\frac{1}{2}$ cup?

FIGURE 5.3

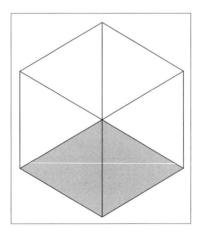

Did you get ⅔, or 1 × ⅓, for both problems? Were your strategies different? Can you tell which problem is quotative and which is partitive?

The first problem is partitive: it is a ratio of ⅔ can to ½ the floor. However, it is difficult to see the distribution, because there isn't even one complete group to deal to, never mind several. The porch floor is the "group," and there is only one half. So we need twice as much paint. With partitive problems, the algorithm of "invert and multiply" as a strategy is usually very apparent. Children notice the multiplying and construct this as a generalized strategy if several similar problems are given and they are asked to explore the relationships they notice. Sometimes, in fact, they multiply so quickly they don't even realize it can be seen as a division problem.

The second problem is quotative, and not just because the context involves measurement. It asks how many times ½ cup goes, or fits, into ⅔ cup. For this problem, learners most often make common denominators. They make the ⅔ cup 4/6 and the ½ cup 3/6. This means the half-cup fits in once with 1/6 left over. But 1/6 of a cup, or 1/6 of the half-cup? There are two wholes: the cup and the half-cup. The whole that matters here is the half-cup, but we are left with 1/6 of the whole cup, so the answer is not 1/6; 1/6 fits into the half-cup three times so it is ⅓ (of the half-cup). This is what makes quotative division problems so difficult for children. The part/whole relationships are critical. Although the relationship with multiplication is not as likely to come up with quotative problems, teachers are usually guaranteed a rich discussion on the big idea of what is the whole.

Generalizing the Models, Generalizing the Operations

Of course, models cannot be transmitted any more than strategies or big ideas can be; learners must construct them. Just because we plan a context with a certain model in mind does not mean that all learners will interpret, or assimilate, the context that way. But it is *likely* that a particular context will affect children's modeling and strategies in a particular way. And it is *likely* that certain types of contexts will generate certain discussions. This is true because it is *likely* that children's initial modeling will be tightly connected to their actions in the context.

In a keynote address at the Exxon Educational Foundation Conference in 1999, Glenda Lappan told about an experience she had had as a teacher. After completing an achievement test, one of her students came up to her and said, "Did you see, the baseball problem was on the test?"

"Well," Glenda said, "I had seen the test, and there was no baseball problem on it. So I asked the girl what she meant. The answer was very informative. This student had recognized that one of the problems could be solved the same way we had solved a problem in class earlier. The class problem had been about baseball. But the test item was not."

This generalizing across problems, across models, and across operations is at the heart of models that are tools for thinking. Models *for* thinking are based on the development of an understanding of part/whole relationships. This includes operations. To have a general model in mind when mathematizing, one has to understand the connection between the problems and the operations (e.g., multiplication and division)—one has to have a generalized notion of each that is not bound to the context.

Let's see how Jake supports this development. Now he has a new landmark on the horizon—*generalizing*. Yet, his children are at many individual points on the landscape. How will he help them all continue their individual journeys yet move them all closer to his new horizon? What will he do next?

"Over the last few days," he begins, "we've been investigating some situations that have involved fractions. You explored how many candy bars you would get if I gave five to every group of six kids. You also made strips for our measuring cups. Before we glue the strips onto our glasses, I would like you to investigate one more thing for homework. Use the strips tonight to revisit and explore the candy bar scenario. Make an entry in your math journal about the relationships you see between the way you solved the candy bar problem and the way you made your strips. Is there any relationship between five bars and six kids sharing them and the strip that includes the five-sixths measurement? Also, write about any other relationships you notice. Tomorrow we'll start math workshop with a discussion of your entries."

What will Jennie, Randy, and Meg do?

Jennie begins by taking the strip that she has divided into thirds. "It's like I used four of these," she writes, and draws a picture again of four candy bars cut into thirds. "Each piece of candy is two inches." She writes 2 above each piece. "Then with the last bar I made 6 pieces. So that's 1 inch of candy more that each kid got." She draws the last bar and writes, "1 more inch for each kid. Each kid gets 5 inches. $2 + 2 + 1$. See." She draws an arrow to a picture of the strip for sixths and shades in $\frac{5}{6}$. She writes, "The problems are related because you can use the strips. They are like candy bars."

In her writing Jennie only notes a superficial relationship: "They [the strips] are like candy bars." However, she has worked out a way, using the strips and her measurements, to add her original fractions, $\frac{2}{3} + \frac{1}{6}$.

Randy writes, "I cut my candy bars up into six pieces and gave each kid five. My strip shows that." He draws the strip with sixths and shades in $\frac{5}{6}$. "When I made my strips today some of my pieces were shorter than Jennie's. It's because I threw some candy away! The problems are related because the answers are the same, $\frac{5}{6}$."

As Randy attempts to connect the two contexts, he resolves his earlier confusion. The context of sharing candy has led him to realize where he went wrong with the strips. Noticing that the problems have the same answer and understanding why and how they are related are two different things, however. It is easy for children to notice that each answer is the same. What is important is that they grapple with the relationships—how it is that five bars divided among six kids results in five sixths of a bar. An important landmark on Jake's horizon is for children to understand the relationships deeply enough that each situation, regardless of the context, can be mathematized with fractions.

Meg illustrates the passing of this landmark when she explains in her math journal, "They are both the same. 5 bars divided by 6 kids is $5 \times \frac{1}{6}$. The $\frac{5}{6}$ mark on the strip is also $5 \times \frac{1}{6}$. The multiplication and the division are related. Fractions are multiplication *and* division!"

As adults having better mathematical understanding, we immediately see the models in the problems, and we expect that the children should. But the models are not in the problems until we mathematize them as such. Children who have not constructed the relationships will mathematize the situations in relation to *their* insights, *their* strategies, *their* ideas. Their modeling at the start will be most often directly linked to their actions in the situation. By inviting the children to compare and reflect on the two different models, Jake is encouraging them to consider relationships.

From Models of Thinking to Models for Thinking

While conversation and reflection on relationships is critical, it is not sufficient to enable all learners to understand—to reach the horizon. If teaching were as easy as involving children in thinking and listening, investigations and children's talk wouldn't even be necessary. Teachers could just explain what they wanted children to learn. All they would have to worry about is motivation, clear communication, and quiet. Unfortunately, genuine teaching and learning are much messier.

To continue the journey, Jake asks his students to explore several other models: ratio tables, double number lines, and arrays. These models are different from the previously described partitive and quotative models and have the potential to become models *for* thinking. Initially, they are part of the context. Jake will use them as a bridge to represent children's thinking. But over time they can become tools for the children to use when modeling, or mathematizing, their lived world. Let's continue observing Jennie, Randy, and Meg.

Ratio Tables

After the children have discussed their journal entries from the night before, Jake begins a new investigation. "I told you that we would be doing a lot of cooking over the next few weeks. That's because I was thinking that we would have a pizza party to raise money for our class. I thought we might make a lot of pizzas and invite people to come to our class for dinner one evening. What do you think of this idea?"

The children excitedly discuss where they will cook all the pizzas, what kind, who will come, etc. Jake explains that he has found a recipe that is easy to make, since no crust is required. He produces the recipe for meat-crust pizzas shown in Figure 5.4. (This activity comes from Encyclopaedia Britannica Educational Corporation, 1997, *Mathematics in Context,* Some of the Parts, p. 16.)

"But that won't be enough for all the people," Katie declares. "I bet they are small. We would need at least one for each person that comes!"

"I know," Jake acknowledges.

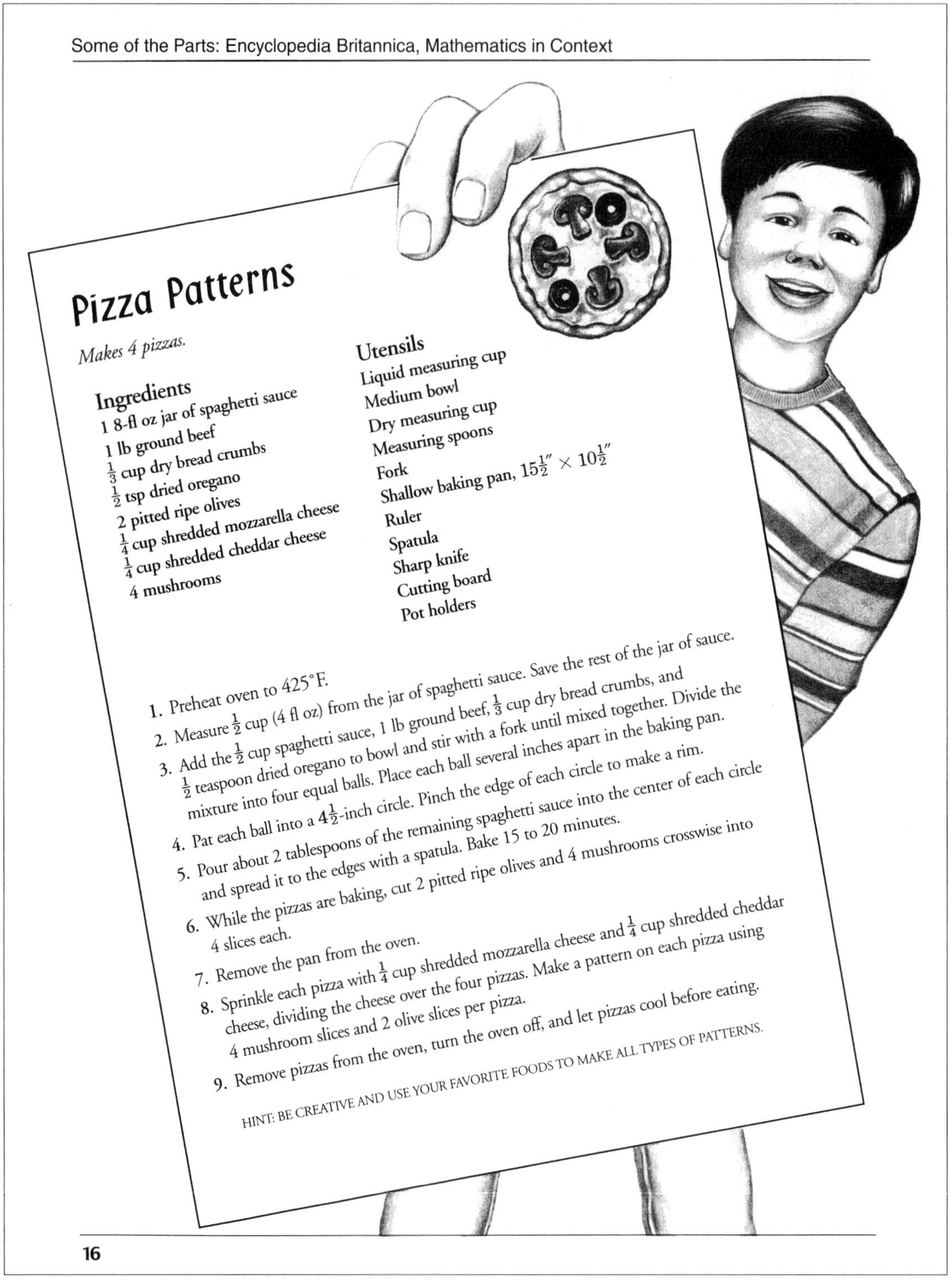

Pizza Patterns

Makes 4 pizzas.

Ingredients
1 8-fl oz jar of spaghetti sauce
1 lb ground beef
$\frac{1}{3}$ cup dry bread crumbs
$\frac{1}{2}$ tsp dried oregano
2 pitted ripe olives
$\frac{1}{4}$ cup shredded mozzarella cheese
$\frac{1}{4}$ cup shredded cheddar cheese
4 mushrooms

Utensils
Liquid measuring cup
Medium bowl
Dry measuring cup
Measuring spoons
Fork
Shallow baking pan, $15\frac{1}{2}'' \times 10\frac{1}{2}''$
Ruler
Spatula
Sharp knife
Cutting board
Pot holders

1. Preheat oven to 425°F.
2. Measure $\frac{1}{2}$ cup (4 fl oz) from the jar of spaghetti sauce. Save the rest of the jar of sauce.
3. Add the $\frac{1}{2}$ cup spaghetti sauce, 1 lb ground beef, $\frac{1}{3}$ cup dry bread crumbs, and $\frac{1}{2}$ teaspoon dried oregano to bowl and stir with a fork until mixed together. Divide the mixture into four equal balls. Place each ball several inches apart in the baking pan.
4. Pat each ball into a $4\frac{1}{2}$-inch circle. Pinch the edge of each circle to make a rim.
5. Pour about 2 tablespoons of the remaining spaghetti sauce into the center of each circle and spread it to the edges with a spatula. Bake 15 to 20 minutes.
6. While the pizzas are baking, cut 2 pitted ripe olives and 4 mushrooms crosswise into 4 slices each.
7. Remove the pan from the oven.
8. Sprinkle each pizza with $\frac{1}{4}$ cup shredded mozzarella cheese and $\frac{1}{4}$ cup shredded cheddar cheese, dividing the cheese over the four pizzas. Make a pattern on each pizza using 4 mushroom slices and 2 olive slices per pizza.
9. Remove pizzas from the oven, turn the oven off, and let pizzas cool before eating.

HINT: BE CREATIVE AND USE YOUR FAVORITE FOODS TO MAKE ALL TYPES OF PATTERNS.

FIGURE 5.4   *Recipe for Meat Crust Pizzas*

"We could double everything," Katie suggests.

"How many pizzas would that make," Jake probes.

Several children respond simultaneously, "Eight."

Jake begins a *ratio table* (see Figure 5.5). "I thought we might make a table like this for different numbers of pizzas. We'll all need to make several. We can send out invitations and have people purchase tickets to know ahead how many we'll need. Then we can work in groups, and each group can be responsible for making a certain number of pizzas. Each group would have a copy of the ratio table to use."

Randy, Jennie, and Meg set to work. Randy immediately doubles, like Kate. "Look we can just keep doing this. So we already know eight. Double that is sixteen, and double that is—thirty-two!" They begin to double each of the ingredients. Most of the fractions are landmark fractions and are thus easy to double. The only one that gives them some trouble is the ⅓.

"One third doubled is two thirds, but what is that doubled?" At first Meg is puzzled. She takes out a set of strips left over after the measuring cups were made and lays out the strip of thirds. "Oh, it's four thirds, and double that is—eight thirds! Hey, that's cool, look. Just the numerator doubles."

Jennie has another idea. "We could just multiply. Like for three times the recipe, twelve pizzas, it's three times the ingredients."

Randy has yet a third idea. "We could add some of these together. Eight and four make twelve. So twelve pizzas would need—one-and-a-half teaspoons of oregano!"

Although Jake introduced the ratio table and recorded Kate's initial response on it, as the children begin to work they use it as a tool for figuring out equivalent ratios. This model of a ratio table will serve them in good stead when they move on to explore the division of fractions. For example, think back to the problem, *I used ⅔ of a can of paint to cover ½ the floor of the porch. How much paint will be needed for the whole floor?* This was pretty easy to solve because of the ½. Doubling is easy. But what if the problem had been ¾ of a can for ⅗ of the porch? Using a ratio table we could easily calculate that ⅕ of the porch used up ¼ of a can. That means ⅖ (the part of the porch undone) needs ½ of a can more. So 1¼ cans should do the whole porch.

	4 pizzas	8 pizzas	... pizzas	
8 fl jar of spaghetti sauce	1			
Ground beef (lb)	1			
Cup dry bread crumbs	1/3			
Tsp dried oregano	½			
Pitted ripe olives	2			

FIGURE 5.5 *Ratio Table*

Double Number Line

Another model that can be used as a powerful calculating tool, particularly in connection with adding and subtracting fractions, is the *double number line*. Once again, let's return to the classroom and watch as Jake introduces it and the children begin to use it.

Every year in Central Park there is a 24 kilometer walk/run for breast cancer research. Jake and the children decide to set up juice stations and distance markers along the way to provide support for the participants.

"Let's set up three juice stations," Jake suggests. "One at the quarter mark, one at the halfway mark, and one at the three-quarter mark. Let's also make distance signs. They could read, you've made it ⅛ of the way, or ⅜ of the way, etc. Or, we could make some that say, four kilometers more to the next juice station. Let's make some plans." As Jake talks, he draws a line to represent the track. At the end, on the top, he writes *24 km*. Underneath the line, but also at the end, he writes *¼, done!*

"Where would the halfway mark be?" Jake turns to the group.

"Twelve k." Several children respond quickly, and Jake writes *12* above the line and *½* under it (see Figure 5.6).

"Let's put in some of the distance markers. Where would one third of the way be?"

Jennie responds. "Eight k. Because three times eight equals twenty-four."

"Everybody agree?" Jake looks around. Seeing no disagreement he goes on. "And one eighth of the race?"

"Three k," Randy offers. "Like Jennie said, three times eight equals twenty-four. That's also eight times three."

"And two eighths?" Jake presses on.

"That's where the juice is," Meg laughs. "We could make a sign at the first marker that says, You've run one eighth of the race; one eighth more to the juice!"

"Suppose we wanted a sign that told people at the one-eighth spot how much more of the race they needed to run to get to the halfway spot?"

"It's two eighths, three eighths—four eighths!" Meg exclaims.

"Four eighths more of the race? Or do you mean one half is the same as four eighths?"

"Oh—yeah." Meg looks puzzled but then offers, "We have to find the difference between one half and one eighth."

Jake writes ½ – ⅛ on the board and turns to the class, "Any ideas?"

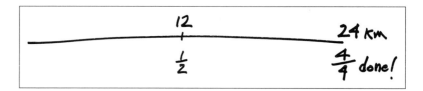

FIGURE 5.6   *The Double Number Line: Kilometers on Top, Fractions Underneath*

"Well, one half is twelve." Randy begins to use the double number line as a tool. "And one eighth is three. So twelve minus three is nine. Nine more k."

"And so what fractional part of the race is that?" Jake asks with a smile.
"Nine twenty-fourths."

Jake adds that to the model he is making.

"Or it could be three eighths," adds Meg. "That's the same."

"Oh, like eighths. Four eighths is one half. So if we are at one eighth, we need three eighths more."

By writing both above and below the line, Jake has created a tool whereby the fractions, in a sense, are turned into whole numbers. On the top of the line, children can compare 12, 3, 9, and 24—whole numbers that represent kilometers. On the bottom, they see the fraction equivalents. The line takes on a double representation, allowing the children to move back and forth as they work. The line becomes a tool to think with. This model is important for adding and subtracting fractions, as we will see in Chapter 7.

Double Number Line and Percentages

The double number line can also be used with percentages. Let's return to Paul Maasen's students in the Netherlands (Chapter 4) as they are investigating percentages and see how he develops it and uses it with his fifth-grade class. His children are about to begin a new investigation, exploring batteries and checking how much power is left.

Paul introduces the power-check battery. "I have some batteries here. Who knows what is special about them?" The students watch Paul with interest, while he shows the batteries. Immediately, they recognize this type of battery.

"You can put your fingers on them and see how much is still left—what percentage," Vincent tells the others. Many of his classmates nod in agreement. "You can check to see how charged up your battery is; whether you have enough power left. Yes, you can see if you can still use it for a long time, or if you need new ones."

On some batteries, a built-in charge tester—like a fuel gauge—tells how long the battery will last. Paul is showing such batteries; you can see the energy gauge fill up when you push on the left and right sides of the battery. So, you can check to see how charged up your battery is; whether you have enough power left.

Most of the students know about these PowerCheck batteries. After all, they use batteries in their Walkman, in their toys, in torches, in clocks . . . To know whether a battery is still charged is important to them.

Paul hands them several batteries and asks them to check whether these are still full. "Press really hard...on the white dots. Both of them. One finger here and one finger there too."

"Does it become yellow?" Arnold asks of his classmate, Lucienne, who is working beside him.

"Yes, but I think that it is very old," Lucienne responds. "See? It becomes yellow. So it's not bad. About half."

Paul continues the investigation. "Well, my Walkman plays for 12 hours on this battery. You can check how full it still is. What I need your help with is to find out how many hours are still left."

Paul walks over to the table where Rudy, Boudewijn, Truus, and Julien are discussing how much of the battery is still charged. On paper, a rectangle represents the gauge on the side of the battery. They shade how full the battery still is and then divide the rectangle into ten parts.

"Well, it's more or less in between." Rudy says. "It is almost three-eighths." Rudy is estimating what part of their drawing is not shaded.

Boudewijn refers to the shaded part and starts to estimate how long the battery will work. "Then this is eight hours," he concludes.

Julien also estimates the hours, "I think it is six hours. If this is half, because here you have just about . . . because, if you have twelve hours, then half is six hours."

The four students are estimating the shaded part in two different ways. On the one hand, they are trying to find out what part is shaded. From this perspective, the whole—the full battery—is 1. On the other hand, they are trying to find out how many hours the battery will still work. From this perspective, the whole—the full battery—is 12 hours. As they work in this context with the batteries, they constantly switch between the hours and the parts. They are learning to switch from one perspective, the battery, to another—the amount of time. And the battery checker provides a real-life context for the development of the double number line because it is a bar that contains both pieces of information.

As the investigation progresses Paul asks the students to notate both pieces of information on drawn bars. On the top is notated how many hours the battery can still last; on the bottom, how full the battery still is (in percentage). To work with this model, Paul uses a sliding percentage strip. In the following excerpt we witness him using it.

"I have a battery that will last for ten hours," Paul declares. The class protests.

"It depends on the brand," James says.

"It depends how expensive they are," Anton adds.

The students discuss how it also depends on the use of the battery; for instance, a clock consumes less energy then a torch. Laughing with his students, Paul refines his statement. "I have a battery here that—fully loaded—will last ten hours in a pocket torch. Okay? It will last ten hours in a torch. What percentage of it is still charged up?" He shows the class the strip with 50 percent (see Figure 5.7). "How long will this battery still last?"

"Fifty . . . fifty percent. So . . . five hours," Fred contributes.

Paul immediately puts the strip on 25 percent (see Figure 5.8). "And this battery? Tim, can you tell what percentage of this battery is still charged up?"

"Two and one half. Two and one half hours, or 25 percent."

"And if the battery is still good for seventy-five percent of its charge?"

"It will last for seven and a half hours."

By using a movable percentage strip, Paul is supporting his students as they work to develop a generalized model, one which they can eventually use as a tool. Originally the model was developed in the context. It was a real battery checker. Now it is becoming more of an abstraction—a paper model of a bar that can be moved. The next step will be to use it in different contexts, and eventually with just bare computation problems. Let's continue to witness this progression.

Several days later, Paul uses the double number line in a minilesson. "Let's start with figuring out ten percent of eight hundred guilders," he begins.

"Eighty, because eight hundred divided by . . . ten times eight . . . a zero is added. It is eight hundred. So you'd get eighty," John replies.

"Twenty percent of eight hundred. Will that be more or less than eighty guilders?" Paul continues.

"It will be more. It will be eighty more," Tina offers.

"Yeah, it will be one hundred sixty," Tim adds.

On the blackboard, Paul has drawn the double number line. He divided the whole line into ten segments and marks two segments of 10 percent. On top he writes *160*, on the bottom he writes *20%*. Although he is drawing a line, not a bar, it is easy for his students to understand the model and the relations on it because of all the work they did with the battery checker, and the sliding percentage strip.

Paul moves to his next problem. "Who knows what thirty percent of eight hundred is?"

Tim replies quickly, "Two hundred forty. You add another eighty."

FIGURE 5.7   *Fifty Percent on the Sliding Percentage Strip*

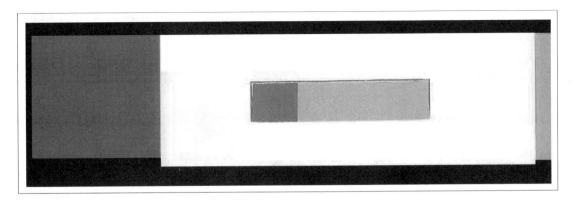

FIGURE 5.8   *Sliding Percentage Strip*

Paul adds another segment to his drawing and marks it with *240* and with *30%*.

"Sixty percent of eight hundred guilders?"

This time Douwe responds. He adds 240 and 240. "First you do thirty. That is two hundred forty. Then you add another two hundred forty and then you have two hundred . . . four hundred . . . four hundred eighty."

Paul paraphrases Douwe's strategy, "So you doubled the thirty percent, and you doubled the money too. That is four hundred eighty."

Julien comments enthusiastically, "I did it differently. You can multiply six times eight. That is forty-eight and then you have to multiply by ten. It is ten times as much."

"And twenty-five percent of eight hundred?" Paul moves to the next problem.

Truus splits the 25 percent into 20 and 5 percent. "First I did the twenty percent. It is one hundred sixty. And then half of ten percent, that is five percent and that is forty. Then you have to add forty to one hundred sixty and that makes two hundred guilders."

"I know a different way," Boudewijn says. "Well, half of half of eight hundred . . . twenty-five percent is one quarter. So you take half of eight hundred. That is four hundred. And then you take half of four hundred. Four hundred is fifty percent. And half of four hundred is twenty-five percent. So it is two hundred guilders."

As Paul continues to work with his students, and as they share various strategies, he records their thinking on a double number line. Even in this short sequence we can see how flexible their thinking is becoming.

The battery checker was a nice context to develop the double number line, but there are also many other realistic situations that can be used. For instance, when downloading or copying a large file on the computer, the download information is given in a kind of double number line (see Figure 5.9). The whole and the amount that is already downloaded are given and the bar shows how much of the whole is downloaded. In our example, almost 40 percent is downloaded.

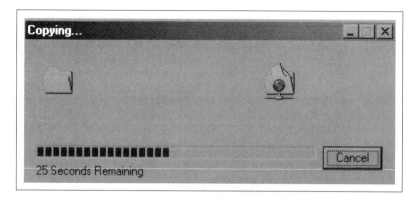

FIGURE 5.9   *Download Information as a Double Number Line*

The Clock

Another helpful model for adding and subtracting fractions like fourths, thirds, sixths, and twelfths is the clock. If children are given the opportunity to explore various ways to represent time, they soon discover that five-minute chunks are twelfths, ten-minute chunks are sixths, fifteen-minute chunks are fourths, etc. Like the double number line, the clock allows children to convert common fractions into whole numbers (minutes), operate with them, and then convert them back to fractions. For example, imagine adding $\frac{1}{3} + \frac{1}{4}$ as 20 minutes plus 15 minutes. The total is 35 minutes, or 7 five-minute chunks. Thus the answer is $\frac{7}{12}$. Or imagine $1\frac{1}{4} - \frac{2}{3}$ as the big hand moving from the forty-minute mark to a quarter after the hour. That is 35 minutes, or once again $\frac{7}{12}$.

Arrays

In volume 2 of this series, we describe how division and multiplication can be modeled with open *arrays*. Their use is no different when multiplying and/or dividing with fractions and/or decimals. For example, Figures 5.10

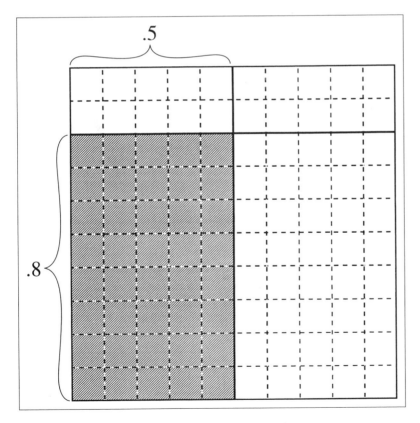

FIGURE 5.10 *Rectangular Plot .8 of a Mile by .5 of a Mile*

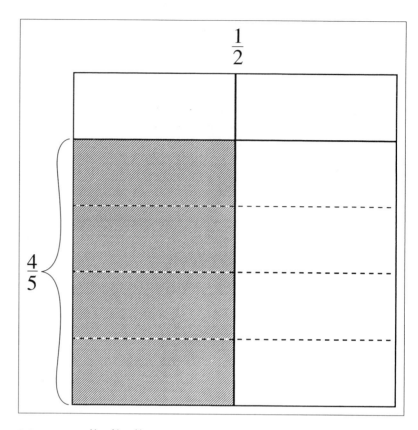

FIGURE 5.11   ⅘ × ½ = ⁴⁄₁₀

and 5.11 show a rectangular plot of land .8 mile by .5 mile, or ⅘ × ½, modeled as an open array.

SUMMING UP . . .

It is impossible to talk about mathematizing without talking about modeling. Mathematical models are mental maps of relationships that can be used as tools when solving problems. These pictures, or mental maps, are powerful. As the well-known scientist and mathematician Sir James Jeans wrote, "The essential fact is that all the pictures that science now draws of nature, and which alone seem capable of according with observational facts, are mathematical pictures." These mental maps depict relationships and help us understand and represent our world.

Models themselves are constructed. They emerge from representations of the *action* in the situation. For example, children don't represent a tree as an object; they represent their actions in relation to the tree. Later these representations of action develop into *representations of the situation* using cubes or drawings. Eventually, modeling develops into a symbolic *representation of the mathematizing itself.* Children represent the *strategies* they used to solve the problem rather than the situation. For example, they may use double number lines or ratio tables to represent their computation strategies. As teachers work with children with models such as the double number line and the ratio table, these representations of their strategies develop into mathematical models of number relationships; they become *mathematical tools.*

The developmental process is characterized by generalization. The importance of generalization in learning cannot be overstated. Piaget (1977) called it "reflective abstraction" and argued that it was the driving force in learning. The mathematician Carl Jacobi, describing his own mathematical thinking process, said, "One should always generalize" (Davis and Hersh 1981). Each developmental shift produces a different way of symbolizing. The model eventually must be able to signify the relationships between numbers and between operations.

At the heart of modeling is number sense—the representation of number relationships. As children construct mental maps of these relationships, they are building powerful tools with which to continue to mathematize their lived world. As Samuel Karlin stated so well, "The purpose of models is not to fit the data, but to sharpen the questions."

Any kind of model (partitive, quotative, ratio table, double number line, clock, or array) must first be developed within rich context investigations. As children use them to envision their world, they also use them to represent their computation strategies. Eventually they become models to think with, as tools.

Arithmetique

Monstrat ars numeri que virtus possit habere
Explico penumeru que sit proportio rerum

6 | ALGORITHMS VERSUS NUMBER SENSE

We are usually convinced more easily by reasons we have found ourselves than by those which have occurred to others.

—*Blaise Pascal*

There still remain three studies suitable for free men. Arithmetic is one of them.

—*Plato*

Try an experiment. Calculate $^6\!/_{16} \times {}^8\!/_{18}$. Don't read on until you have an answer.

If you are like most people who are a product of the American school system, you probably got a pencil and paper, wrote the numbers down, and performed the following algorithm for multiplication of fractions. First you multiplied the numerators to get forty-eight. Then you multiplied the denominators (rewriting the multiplication vertically and performing the multiplication algorithm for whole numbers) to get 288. These actions resulted in the fraction $^{48}\!/_{288}$, which you then reduced to $^1\!/_6$ (perhaps even using several steps here). To check yourself, you probably went back and repeated the same actions and calculations; if you got the same answer twice, you assumed your calculations were correct.

Now take out a piece of graph paper and draw a rectangle. Use this rectangle to show the multiplication that represents the problem and what you did. See if you can find the rectangular arrays that represent the problems you did as you calculated the forty-eight and the 288, and then show in this rectangle the equivalence involved in reducing this fraction to $^1\!/_6$. If this is difficult for you, the way the algorithm was taught to you has worked against your own conceptual understanding of multiplication.

The algorithms for multiplying fractions are very difficult for children to understand. Why? Well, just think how nonsensical these steps must seem to them. They are struggling to understand what fractions even mean. Furthermore, they have often been taught—and therefore understand—the operation of multiplication as repeated addition, and they struggle to find the repeated addition when multiplying fractions. Finally, as they treat the numbers in the numerators and denominators as digits to perform the algorithm, they lose sight of the quantities they are actually multiplying and make any number of errors in calculating each of the separate pieces.

Liping Ma (1999) compared the way Chinese and American teachers think about and teach the multiplication algorithms and how they work with children who make place value mistakes. Most Chinese teachers approach the teaching of the multiplication algorithms conceptually.

For the whole number algorithm, they explain the distributive property and break the problem up into the component problems: $16 \times 18 = (10 + 6) \times (10 + 8) = (6 \times 8) + (6 \times 10) + (10 \times 8) + (10 \times 10) = 48 + 60 + 80 + 100$. Once this conceptual understanding is developed, they associate the steps in the algorithm with the component parts in the equation. (Figure 6.1 shows these steps as rectangles within the larger array of 16×18.) In contrast, 70 percent of American teachers teach this algorithm as a series of procedures and interpret children's errors as a problem with carrying and lining up. They remind children of the "rules"—that they are multiplying by tens and therefore have to move their answer to the next column. To help children follow the "rules" correctly, they often use lined paper and suggest that children use zero as a placeholder.

To teach the multiplication algorithm for fractions, Chinese teachers again approach it conceptually, focusing on both the distributive and the associative properties. They might explain that $\frac{6}{16}$ is equivalent to $6 \times \frac{1}{16}$ and $\frac{8}{18}$ is equivalent to $8 \times \frac{1}{18}$ and that therefore $\frac{6}{16} \times \frac{8}{18}$ is equivalent to $6 \times 8 \times \frac{1}{16} \times \frac{1}{18}$, or $48 \times \frac{1}{288}$. In contrast, American teachers are more likely to teach it procedurally, with rules like multiply the numerators, then the denominators, then reduce.

FIGURE 6.1
16 × 18 = 288
Components of the
Algorithm

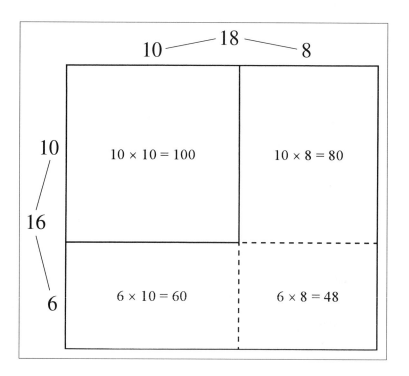

One could argue that if we taught the algorithms conceptually, as Li-ping Ma advocates, more understanding would develop. This is probably true. But should the algorithm be the goal of computation instruction? In today's world, do we want learners to have to rely on paper and pencil? Is the algorithm the fastest, most efficient way to compute? When are algorithms helpful? When does one pull out a calculator? What does it mean to compute with number sense?

Ann Dowker (1992) asked forty-four mathematicians to do several typical multiplication and division computation problems and assessed their strategies. Only 4 percent of the responses, across all the problems and across all the mathematicians, were solved with algorithms. The mathematicians looked at the numbers first, then found efficient strategies that fit well with the numbers. They made the numbers friendly, and they played with relationships. Interestingly, they also varied their strategies, sometimes using different strategies for the same problems when they were asked about them on different days! They appeared to pick a strategy that seemed appropriate to the numbers and that was prevalent in their minds at that time; they searched for efficiency and elegance of solution; they made numbers friendly (often by using landmark numbers); and they found the process creative and enjoyable.

How might mathematicians solve $\frac{6}{16} \times \frac{8}{18}$? There are many ways. One could, for example, swap the numerators. This makes the problem $\frac{8}{16} \times \frac{6}{18}$, or reduced to $\frac{1}{2} \times \frac{1}{3}$: the answer this way can be arrived at mentally. Why does this work? What does it mean to multiply $\frac{6}{16}$ by $\frac{8}{18}$? Figure 6.2 shows

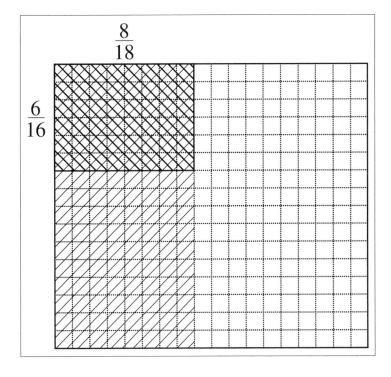

FIGURE 6.2
$\frac{6}{16} \times \frac{8}{18}$
A patio, 16 feet by 18 feet. $\frac{8}{18}$ of the tiles have been laid so far and $\frac{6}{16}$ of these have been mortared in place.

this multiplication in a rectangular array. Imagine square tiles being laid to build a patio, 16 feet by 18 feet. Next, imagine that $\frac{8}{18}$ of the tiles (8 out of 18 columns) have been laid so far and that $\frac{6}{16}$ of *these* (6 out of 16 rows) have been mortared in place. The small rectangular area that is now complete is a 6-by-8 array (48 tiles). This small array fits into the larger 16-by-18 array (288 tiles) six times. Thus, $\frac{6}{16} \times \frac{8}{18} = \frac{1}{6}$.

Now look at this in a different way. Imagine the smaller array turned 90 degrees: it now has 6 columns and 8 rows (see Figure 6.3). The relationship to the whole is still the same, but the problem is now $\frac{8}{16} \times \frac{6}{18}$, or $\frac{1}{2} \times \frac{1}{3}$, which of course is easily calculated mentally. Swapping numerators and reducing if needed is a powerful mental math strategy that is often helpful. For example, try it with $\frac{4}{6} \times \frac{3}{7}$, or $\frac{1}{3} \times \frac{5}{8}$. The first problem becomes $\frac{1}{2} \times \frac{4}{7}$, or $\frac{2}{7}$. The second becomes $\frac{5}{3} \times \frac{1}{8}$, or $\frac{1}{2}$. And it is easy to see in arrays how the smaller rectangular array, formed by the numerators, just gets turned: $(4 \times \frac{1}{7}) \times (3 \times \frac{1}{6})$ as $(4 \times 3) \times (\frac{1}{6} \times \frac{1}{7})$ or as $(4 \times \frac{1}{7}) \times (3 \times \frac{1}{6})$. See Figures 6.4a–6.4c.

This strategy is of course only helpful in some cases. But there are many wonderful mental math strategies if one has a deep understanding of number and operation. Calculating with number sense, as a mathematician, means having many strategies at your disposal, and looking to the numbers first, *before* choosing a strategy. Let's look at a few other strategies.

How about getting rid of fractions altogether? For $3\frac{1}{2} \times 14$, we could double the $3\frac{1}{2}$ to get rid of the fraction and thus halve the 14—turning the

FIGURE 6.3
$\frac{8}{16} \times \frac{6}{18}$

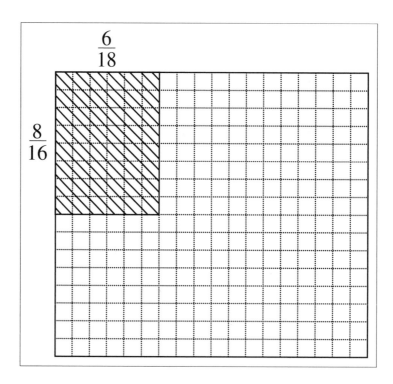

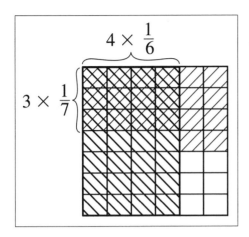

FIGURE 6.4a
(3 × 1/7) × (4 × 1/6)

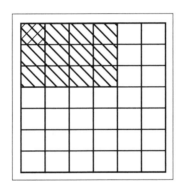

FIGURE 6.4b
(3 × 4) × (1/6 × 1/7)

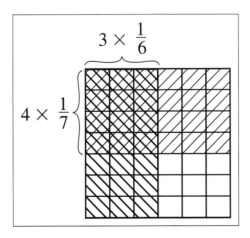

FIGURE 6.4c
(4 × 1/7) × (3 × 1/6)

problem into 7×7! Now we have the answer of 49 mentally. For $2\frac{1}{4} \times 16$, we could get rid of the fraction by multiplying $2\frac{1}{4}$ by 4 and dividing the 16 by 4. This turns the problem into 9×4, or 36. Try using this strategy to compute $3\frac{1}{5} \times 45$. Did you get rid of the fraction by multiplying $3\frac{1}{5}$ by 5? Great! And then you divided 45 by 5? Great! Now you have 16×9. We could keep on doubling and halving. $16 \times 9 = 8 \times 18 = 4 \times 36 = 2 \times 72 = 144$! Or, since we know that $16 \times 10 = 160$, all we have to do is subtract the extra 16 to get the answer of 144.

We can also use this strategy to get rid of decimals. How about $.8 \times 350$? If we multiply the .8 by 10 and divide the 350 by 10, we turn the problem into 8×35. Halving and doubling, we get 4×70: 280! Or we could think of .8 as $\frac{4}{5}$, turning the decimal into a fraction; $\frac{1}{5}$ of 350 is 70; once again we get 4×70. All of these strategies work because of the associative property of multiplication. We can do whatever we want first to make the problems easier:

$$.8 \times 350 = ?$$

$$.8 \times 350 = 4 \times 70 = 280$$

$$.8 \times 350 = (8 \times \tfrac{1}{10}) \times (10 \times 35)$$
$$= 8 \times (\tfrac{1}{10} \times 10) \times 35 = \times 4 \times 2 \times 35$$

$$.8 \times 350 = \tfrac{4}{5} \times 350 = (4 \times \tfrac{1}{5}) \times 350 = 4 \times (\tfrac{1}{5} \times 350)$$

Note how all of these alternative, creative ways can be done so quickly—in most cases mentally. If paper and pencil are used, it is only to keep track. Playing with numbers like this is based on a deep understanding of number, landmark numbers, properties, and operations. And it characterizes true number sense. In contrast, a child who is taught to use the algorithm to multiply $.8 \times 350$ stops thinking. He sacrifices the relationships in order to treat the numbers as digits. And any teacher of middle school children will attest to the difficulties children have as they try to complete each of the multiplication pieces, carry appropriately, and determine where the decimal point goes in the answer.

Algorithms can be very helpful when multiplying or dividing large, nonfriendly numbers, or when working with messy fractions that can't easily be simplified. But in today's world, isn't that when we take out the calculator anyway? If we have to reach for paper and pencil to perform the arithmetic, why not reach for the calculator?

THE HISTORY OF ALGORITHMS

Through time and across cultures many different algorithms have been used for multiplication. For example, for many years Egyptians used an algorithm based on doubling. To multiply 28×12 (or 12×28), they would calculate

$1 \times 28 = 28$, $2 \times 28 = 56$, $4 \times 28 = 112$, $8 \times 28 = 224$, and so on. As soon as they had calculations for numbers that added up to the original multiplier (in this case 12), they would stop doubling and add: here, $8 + 4 = 12$, therefore 112 and 224 added together (336) equals 12×28.

Russian peasants used a halving and doubling algorithm. To multiply 28×12, they would first halve the 28 and double the 12, getting 14×24. Next they would repeat the procedure, getting 7×48. When an odd number (like 7 in this case) appeared, resulting in a remainder when halved, they would round down, thus using 3 (instead of $3\frac{1}{2}$) $\times$ 96 and 1 (instead of $1\frac{1}{2}$) $\times$ 192. They continued halving and doubling until they reached the last problem in the series ($1 \times n$), in this case 1×192. Then they added up all the factors with odd multipliers—$48 + 96 + 192$ in this case—and arrived at the answer—$28 \times 12 = 336$.

In the early part of the ninth century, the great Arab mathematician Muhammad ibn Musa al-Khwarizmi invented the algorithms for multiplication and division that we teach in most schools today. (In Latin his name was Algorismus—hence the term *algorithm*.) Their beauty was that they were generalized procedures that could be used as efficient computation strategies for all problems—even messy ones with many digits. During this time, calculations using large numbers were needed both in the marketplace and for merchants' accounting purposes. Because calculations on the abacus were actions, there was no written record of the arithmetic, only the answer. And only the intelligentsia, practiced in the art of the abacus, could calculate.

Denis Guedj (1996) describes a bit of the history:

> In the Middle Ages computations were carried out on an abacus, also called a computing table, a calculating device resembling a table with columns or ruled horizontal lines; digits were represented by counters, or apices. From the twelfth century on, this type of abacus was progressively replaced by the dust board as a tool of calculations. This development did not come about without a struggle between those who, evoking the ancient Greek mathematician Pythagoras, championed the abacus and those who became masters of algorism, the new Arabic number system. In this competition between the Ancients and Moderns, the former saw themselves as the keepers of the secrets of the art of computation and the defenders of the privileges of the guild of professional calculators . . . [while] the new system indisputably marked the democratization of computation. (53–54)

With the invention of the algorithms and the dissemination of multiplication tables to use while performing them, even the most complex computations were possible, and written records of the calculations could be kept.

Schools soon set about to teach the procedures. In the Renaissance in Europe the manipulation of numbers and the practice of arithmetic were signs of advanced learning; those who knew how to multiply and divide with algorithms were guaranteed a professional career. In the Musee de Cluny, in Paris, there is a sixteenth-century tapestry depicting Lady Arithmetic teaching the new calculation methods to gilded youth. (A photograph of this is used as the lead photo in this chapter.)

But today's world is different. Human beings have continued through the centuries to design and build tools with which to calculate, from the slide rule, in 1621, to the first mechanical calculator, invented by Pascal in 1642, to the handheld calculator, in 1967, to today's graphic calculators. The World Wide Web even provides virtual calculators (Guedj 1996). Difficult computations, originally solved by algorithms, are now done with these tools.

There have also been many different algorithms for computation with fractions. As described in Chapter 3, in the Stone Age there was no need for fractions; fractions seem to have developed during the Bronze Age. Egyptians during this period recognized only unit fractions (fractions with numerators of one) and the fraction $\frac{2}{3}$. Thus they would have understood the fractions $\frac{6}{16}$ or $\frac{8}{18}$ only as six loaves shared with sixteen people and eight loaves shared with eighteen people, representing $\frac{6}{16}$ as $\frac{1}{3} + \frac{1}{24}$ and $\frac{8}{18}$ as $\frac{1}{3} + \frac{1}{6}$. Adding or subtracting these amounts is easy. No common denominators are needed. You just string all the unit fractions together: $\frac{1}{3} + \frac{1}{24} + \frac{1}{3} + \frac{1}{6} = \frac{2}{3} + \frac{1}{6} + \frac{1}{24}$.

Fractions were multiplied by doubling (or tripling) one of the denominators and divided by doubling (or tripling) one of the numerators. For example, to multiply $\frac{1}{2} \times \frac{1}{3}$, one would just double the 3 or triple the 2 to get an answer of $\frac{1}{6}$. To multiply $\frac{1}{4} \times \frac{1}{3}$, one would double the 3 twice since $\frac{1}{4}$ is half of $\frac{1}{2}$—the 3 becomes 6, then the 6 becomes 12. Thus the answer is $\frac{1}{12}$. To divide $\frac{1}{3}$ by $\frac{1}{2}$, one would double the numerator. Thus the answer is $\frac{2}{3}$. To multiply $\frac{6}{16} \times \frac{8}{18}$, the problem at the beginning of this chapter, Egyptians would have used the distributive property and done the following: $(\frac{1}{3} + \frac{1}{24}) \times (\frac{1}{3} + \frac{1}{6}) = \frac{1}{9} + \frac{1}{27} + \frac{1}{72} + \frac{1}{216}$. Imagine how difficult it would be to do very complex problems with the Egyptian algorithm!

Had Mesopotamian mathematics, like that of the Nile Valley, been based on the addition of integers and unit fractions, we might not have seen decimal calculations until the Renaissance! However, their neighbors, the Babylonians (as also described in Chapter 3), had developed a base-*sixty* number system. They used this to represent fractional amounts, *sexagesimals*. Knowledge of how place value could be used allowed the Babylonians to do all their calculating of fractions in the same way as they did whole numbers, taking care of the decimal (really, sexagesimal) point only at the end.

The handheld calculator has now replaced paper-and-pencil algorithms. Does this mean we don't need to know how to calculate? Of course not. To be successful in today's world, we need a deep conceptual understanding of mathematics. We are bombarded with numbers, statistics, advertisements, and similar data every day—on the radio, on television, and in newspapers. We need good mental ability and good number sense in order to evaluate advertising claims, estimate quantities, efficiently calculate the numbers we deal with every day and judge whether these calculations are reasonable, add up restaurant checks and determine equal shares, interpret data and statistics, and so on. We need to be able to move back and forth from fractions to decimals to percents. We need a much deeper sense of number and operation than ever before—one that allows us to both estimate and make exact calculations mentally. How do we, as teachers, develop children's ability to do this? How do we engage them in being young mathematicians at work?

TEACHING FOR NUMBER SENSE

Each day at the start of math workshop, Dawn Selnes, a fifth-grade teacher in New York City, does a short minilesson on computation strategies. She usually chooses five or six related problems and asks the children to solve them and share their strategies with one another. Crucial to her choice of problems is the relationship between them. She picks problems that are likely to lead to a discussion of a specific strategy. She allows her students to construct their own strategies by decomposing numbers in ways that make sense to them. Posted around the room are signs the children have made throughout the year as they have developed a repertoire of strategies for operations with fractions. One reads, "Make use of tens"; another, "Halves & doubles"; a third, "Get rid of the fraction"; a fourth, "Use all the factors in pretty ways."

On the chalkboard today is the string of problems the children are discussing. Although the string ends with fractions, it begins with a few whole number multiplication problems, and Alice is describing how she solved 9×30. "I just used all the factors," she explains. "I thought of it as nine times three times ten. I knew that nine times three was twenty-seven, so times ten is two hundred and seventy."

Dawn asks for other strategies, but most of the children have treated the problem similarly, so Dawn goes to the next problem in her string, 15×18. Several children use the distributive property here. Tom's strategy is representative of many, and several children nod in agreement as he explains how he did 10×18 and got 180, and then took half of that to figure out the answer to 5×18. He completes the calculation by adding 180 to 90, for an answer of 270. Lara's strategy is similar, if not as elegant, but it makes sense to her. She multiplies using tens, too, but she breaks up the eighteen instead of the fifteen and multiplies 10×15, and then 8×15. These two products together also result in 270.

Ned agrees with their answer but with a smile he says, "Yeah, but you didn't even have to calculate. It's the same as nine times thirty, because the thirty is halved, and the nine is doubled!"

Although all the children in the class are comfortable with this doubling and halving strategy and understand why it works (having explored it thoroughly with arrays earlier in the year), they have not all thought to use it, because Dawn has turned the numbers around. It might have been more obvious if she had written 18 × 15 directly underneath 9 × 30. But she wants to challenge them to think.

Now Dawn moves to fractions. She writes 4½ × 60 as the third problem. Several children immediately raise their hands, but Dawn waits for those still working to finish. Alice is one of them, so she asks her to share first. "What did you do, Alice?"

"I split it into four times sixty first," Alice begins, "and I did that by doing four times six equals twenty-four. Then times ten is two hundred and forty. Then I knew that a half of sixty was thirty. So thirty plus two hundred and forty is two hundred and seventy."

"My way is kind of like yours," another classmate, Daniel, responds, "but I subtracted."

"But then you would get the wrong answer," Alice tells him, looking puzzled.

"No, what I mean is I did five times six times ten. That was three hundred. Then I subtracted the thirty."

"Where did you get the five?" Several of his classmates are also now puzzled.

"That was easier for me than four and a half. But that's why I took thirty away at the end," Daniel explains, very proud of his strategy.

Dawn checks to see whether everyone understands by asking who can paraphrase Daniel's strategy. Several children do so, and Dawn seems satisfied that the group appears to understand. "That's a really neat strategy, isn't it?" Daniel beams, and Dawn turns to Ned, "And what did you do Ned? Your hand was up so quickly. Did you see a relationship to another problem again?"

Ned laughs, "Yep. Just doubling and halving again. It's the same as nine times thirty. The nine was halved and the thirty was doubled."

Several children make surprised exclamations. Dawn smiles and goes to the next problem: 2¼ × 120. This time everyone's hand is up quickly, and Dawn calls on Tanya, who has not yet shared. Tanya, as well as the rest of the class, has made use of the doubling and halving relationships in this string of problems.

The other strategies that have previously been offered are also powerful strategies, and Dawn does not want to imply that they should be replaced by doubling and halving. She is only trying to help her children think about relationships in problems, to look to the problems *first* before calculating. To ensure that this happens she follows with the next two problems: 15 × 36, then 15½ × 36. For the first, most students see the relationship between it and 30 × 18. Since they have already calculated 15 × 18, they know they just need to double that answer. A few children solve it by doing 10 × 36 to get 360, halving that to get 180, and then adding these partial products for an answer of 540. For the second problem everyone uses the distributive property, adding 18 more for an answer of 558.

Dawn ends her string with a very difficult problem: $15\frac{1}{2} \times 4\frac{1}{2}$. She asks the children to write their strategy and solution down in their math journal and then to turn to the person sitting next to them on the rug and share it. What strategies will the children use? How solid is their understanding? Most complete the problem successfully, but not all children finish, and some make calculation errors. But they show a rich variety of strategies that are evidence of deep understanding and good number sense (see Figure 6.5).

These young mathematicians are composing and decomposing flexibly as they multiply fractions. They are inventing their own strategies. They are looking for relationships between the problems. They are looking at the numbers first before they decide on a strategy.

Children don't do this automatically. Dawn has developed this ability in her students by focusing on computation during minilessons with strings of related problems every day. She has developed the big ideas and models through investigations, but once this understanding has been constructed, she hones computation strategies in minilessons such as this one.

Traditionally, mathematics educators thought teaching for number sense meant helping children connect their actions to real objects. We used

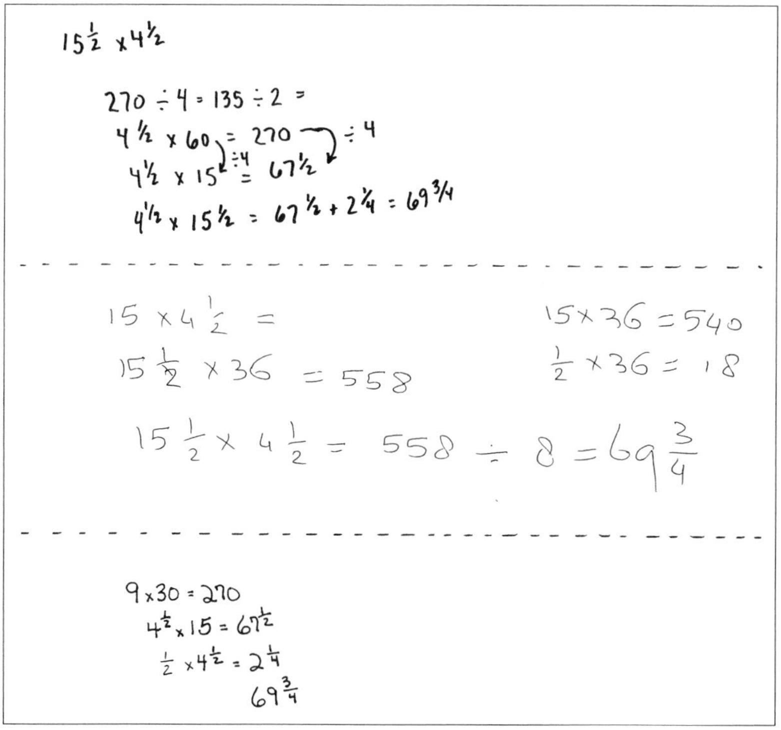

FIGURE 6.5 *$15\frac{1}{2} \times 4\frac{1}{2}$: Three Different Children's Strategies*

base-ten blocks and trading activities to help children understand regrouping. We built arrays with base-ten materials and looked at the dimensions and the area. We used Cuisennaire rods and fraction strips to develop a connection for children between the actions of regrouping the objects, making equivalent fractions, and the symbolic notation in the algorithms. We talked about the connection between the concrete, the pictorial, and the symbolic. But all of these pedagogical techniques were used to teach the algorithms. The goal of arithmetic teaching was algorithms, albeit with understanding.

In the 1980s, educators began to discuss whether the goal of arithmetic computation should be algorithms at all. Constance Kamii's research has led her to insist that teaching algorithms is in fact harmful to children's mathematical development (Kamii and Dominick 1998). First, she examined children's invented procedures for whole number multiplication and division and found that children's procedures for multiplication always went from left to right, from the largest units to the smallest. With division, children's

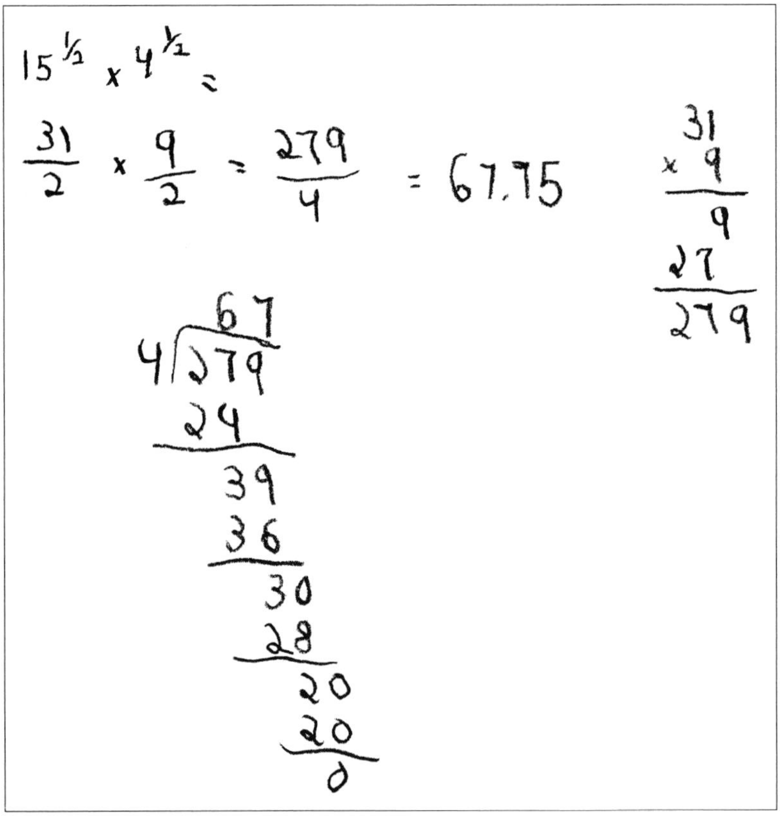

FIGURE 6.6   *15½ × 4½: One Child's Attempt at the Algorithm*

procedures went from the smallest units to the largest, from right to left. Yet the algorithms require opposite procedures: with multiplication one starts with the units and works right to left; with division, one starts with the largest unit (hundreds, for example) and works right to left.

Is the situation any different with fractions? Only one child in Dawn's class used the algorithm, and he had been taught it at home. He turned the problem into $3\frac{1}{2} \times \frac{9}{2} = \frac{279}{4}$ (see Figure 6.6). This procedure was obviously difficult for him, and he made many errors along the way. We might also wonder if he knows why this procedure works. When algorithms are taught as procedures to use for any and all problems, children necessarily give up their own meaning making in order to perform them. The algorithms hinder children's ability to construct an understanding of the distributive and associative properties of multiplication, which underlie algebraic computation. And worse, they require that children see themselves as proficient users of someone else's mathematics, not as mathematicians.

Kamii's data and her strong arguments from a developmental perspective are convincing, and many educators have begun to allow children to construct their own computation strategies. This isn't enough, however. Although their invented strategies do become more efficient over time, these strategies are remarkably similar, and many of them are cumbersome and inefficient.

Over the last seven years or so Mathematics in the City has looked seriously at how to develop in students a repertoire of efficient computation strategies that are based on a deep understanding of number sense and operation and that honor children's own constructions. The next chapter describes the techniques we have been using and the strategies we try to develop for fraction and decimal computation.

SUMMING UP . . .

Algorithms were developed in the Middle Ages by the Arab mathematician al-Khwarizmi. There was also a long period when computations were performed with unit fractions and/or sexagesimals before common fraction algorithms became accepted. The use of algorithms brought about a democratization of computation; people no longer had to rely on the select few who were competent users of the abacus. When algorithms appeared, there was political tension between those who wanted to hold on to the abacus and those who wanted to learn the new methods. Interestingly, a similar political situation exists today. As schools have begun to reform their teaching, as algorithms have been replaced with mental math strategies and calculating with number sense, arguments have broken out between those who fight to maintain the "old" math and those who favor reform. Many newspaper articles play into the fear that children will not be able to compute. This fear is based on uninformed, often mistaken, notions of the reform. Parents are products of the old education, and therefore they define mathematics as the skills they were taught. When they don't see their children learning what they believe to be the goals of mathematics—the algorithms—they assume that nothing is being learned. Many of them have called the new mathematics "fuzzy" or "soft" and described it as a "dumbing down."

Algorithms—a structured series of procedures that can be used across problems, regardless of the numbers—do have an important place in mathematics. After students have a deep understanding of number relationships and operations and have developed a repertoire of computation strategies, they may find it interesting to investigate why the traditional computation algorithms work. Exploring strategies that can be used with larger, messy numbers when a calculator is not handy is an interesting inquiry—one in which the traditional algorithms can be employed. In these inquiries algorithms can surface as a formal, generalized procedure—an alternative approach to use when the numbers are not nice. Often algorithms come up in classroom discussions, too, because parents have taught them to their children and children attempt to use them without understanding why they work. Exploring them and figuring out why they work may deepen children's understanding.

Algorithms should not be the primary goal of computation instruction, however. Using algorithms, the same series of steps with all problems, is antithetical to calculating with number sense. Calculating with number sense means that one should look at the numbers first and then decide on a strategy that is fitting—and efficient. Developing number sense takes time; algorithms taught too early work against the development of good number sense. Children who learn to think, rather than to apply the same procedures by rote regardless of the numbers, will be empowered. They will not see mathematics as a dogmatic, dead discipline, but as a living, creative one. They will thrive on inventing their own rules, because these rules will serve afterward as the foundation for solving other problems.

By abandoning the rote teaching of algorithms, we are not asking children to learn less, we are asking them to learn more. We are asking them to mathematize, to think like mathematicians, to look at the numbers before they calculate. To paraphrase Plato, we are asking children to approach mathematics as "free men and women." Children can and do construct their own strategies, and when they are allowed to make sense of calculations in their own ways, they understand better. In the words of the mathematician, Blaise Pascal, "We are usually convinced more easily by reasons we have found ourselves than by those which have occurred to others."

In focusing on number sense, we are also asking teachers to think mathematically. We are asking them to develop their own mental math strategies in order to develop them in their students. Once again teachers are on the edge, not only the edge between the structure and development of mathematics, but also the edge between the old and the new—between the expectations of parents and the expectations of the new tests and the new curricula.

The backlash is strong, and walking this edge is difficult. Teachers need support. Learning to teach in a way that supports mathematizing—in a way that supports calculating with number sense—takes time. Sometimes, parents have responded by hiring tutors to teach their children the algorithms—a solution that has often been detrimental to children as they grapple to understand number and operation. Sometimes, as teachers have attempted to reform their practice, children have been left with no algorithms and no repertoire of strategies, only their own informal, inefficient inventions. The reform will fail if we do not approach calculation seriously, if we do not produce children who can calculate efficiently. Parents will define our success in terms of the their old notions of mathematics. They saw the goal of arithmetic, of school mathematics, as calculation. They will look for what they know, for what they learned, for what they define as mathematics.

7 | DEVELOPING EFFICIENT COMPUTATION WITH MINILESSONS

I think, therefore I am. . . . Each problem that I solved became a rule which served afterwards to solve other problems.

—René Descartes

Mathematics is the only instructional material that can be presented in an entirely undogmatic way.

—Max Dehn

MINILESSONS WITH MENTAL MATH STRINGS

"I saw three groups of four, and there's two rows of them, so I know it's twenty-four." Deena, a New York City fifth grader, is explaining what she has just seen. Risa Lasher, her teacher, is beginning math workshop, as she normally does each day, with a short ten- or fifteen-minute minilesson focusing on computation strategies. Using an overhead projector, Risa has displayed, for a few seconds, the image shown in Figure 7.1. The children, who are all sitting on the rug in the meeting area with her, have been asked to talk to their neighbor about what they have seen.

Suzanne, sitting next to Deena says, "I agree, but I saw them as two groups of three on top and two on the bottom. That was my twelve. But then I doubled twelve, too—because it repeated." Darius and Sasha, on the other hand, have counted the groups of three and multiplied, 3×8; others have calculated the total differently still.

Risa starts a whole-group discussion. "Deena and Suzanne, I overheard you two saying that you saw two groups of four times three." On the overhead transparency Risa writes $2 \times (4 \times 3) = 24$. "Does this represent what you saw?"

Deena and Suzanne agree. "But we each saw the four times three differently," Deena explains as she goes to the chalkboard where the image is again being projected. She draws a circle around the top row, which she has used;

and then with a different-color chalk, she circles the four groups Suzanne has used.

"And Darius and Sasha, how did you two see it?" Risa continues the conversation.

"We just saw eight groups of three," Sasha responds for both of them. Risa writes $8 \times 3 = 24$ and then asks, "Any other ways? Juan?"

"I saw two threes as a group of six," Juan explains, continuing with how he then just did 4×6. Risa writes the equation $4 \times (2 \times 3) = 24$ on the overhead transparency as well and ensures that what she has written represents Juan's thinking.

He agrees that it does, so Risa segues into a discussion of fractions. "So there are a lot of ways to calculate the whole here. What if I just circle these three? Could we think about this amount as a fraction? What part of the whole is it?"

"If the whole is twenty-four, then what you circled is three twenty-fourths, three out of twenty-four," offers David, proudly showing what he knows about fractions.

"But there are other ways, too," Deena asserts. "It's also one eighth."

"Why?"

"Because if you count each group of three as one group, then it is one group out of eight," Deena explains clearly.

David at first looks surprised but then is intrigued. He is now seeing both perspectives. "What is it one eighth of, David?" Risa asks, attempting to deepen his understanding.

"It's one eighth of—twenty-four?" David responds a bit tentatively.

"What do the rest of you think? Do you agree with David?"

Marta, who has been rather quiet until now, raises her hand and offers, "I agree with him. It is one eighth of twenty-four—because that is three—because twenty-four divided by eight equals three."

"You've said a lot there, Marta," Risa responds. "Let me write down all the equations that have been mentioned so far and let's see how they are related." Risa turns off the overhead, erases the board, and writes the following string of equations:

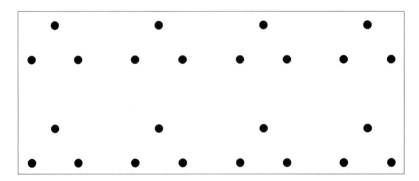

FIGURE 7.1   *Groups of Dots*

$$^3\!/_{24} = \frac{1}{8}$$

$$\frac{1}{8} \text{ of } 24 = 3$$

$$^3\!/_{24} \text{ of } 24 = 3$$

$$^{24}\!/_8 = 3$$

$$8 \times 3 = 24$$

$$4 \times 6 = 24$$

$$2 \times 12 = 24$$

Then she suggests, "Turn to the person you are sitting next to and talk about the relationships you see in this string of equations." Risa uses this technique so that everyone will be involved; she hopes to get all her students to reflect on the *underlying big ideas.* She succeeds.

"What we talked about," Suzanne begins when Risa reopens the whole-group discussion, "is that they're related because multiplication and division are related."

"Tell us more. How so?" Risa probes.

"Well, like—there are eight groups of three. So that is twenty-four over eight equals three, but it is also one eighth of twenty-four equals three, because eight times three equals twenty-four."

Maria, who has been talking with Marta, chimes in, "Yeah, and you could do one third of twenty-four, too. That would be eight!"

Risa adds this equation to the string and asks, "Any other ideas?"

Paul, David's discussion partner, elaborates. "It's like the one is the three and eight is the whole. But twenty-four is also the whole—so it's one eighth of twenty-four equals three, but it's also one eighth equals three twenty-fourths."

"Could we make more related equations for the last two problems, four times six equals twenty-four and two times twelve equals twenty-four?"

David offers $\frac{1}{4} \times 24 = 6$ and $\frac{1}{6} \times 24 = 4$. Juan suggests $^4\!/_{24} = \frac{1}{6}$. Risa adds these equations to the string and comments, "And there are more, too, aren't there? It's really cool how division and multiplication relationships help us think about fractions."

In this brief minilesson, Risa has succeeded in bringing to the fore some important big ideas: the connection between multiplication and division and the fact that although the whole may change, the relationship between the parts and whole must stay constant for fractions to be equivalent. Usually each day, at the start of math workshop, Risa chooses a string of four or five related problems and asks her students to solve them. Together they discuss and compare strategy efficiency and explore relationships between problems, just as Dawn did with her children in the previous chapter. Today, however, Risa helped her students generate a string of related problems rather than presenting one herself. Whether students generate the string or solve a given string prepared by a teacher, the relationships between the problems are the critical element.

Good minilessons always focus on problems that are likely to develop certain strategies or big ideas that are landmarks on the landscape of learning. We call these groups of problems *strings* because they are a structured series (a string) of computations that are related in such a way as to develop and highlight number relationships and operations. Designing such strings and other minilessons to develop computation strategies requires a deep understanding of number and operation; the choice of numbers and the models and contexts used are not random.

CHOOSING THE STRATEGIES, CHOOSING THE NUMBERS, CHOOSING THE MODELS

Finding a Familiar, Landmark Whole

The quick image that Risa chose was designed to prompt a discussion about the relationship between multiplication and division—an important idea by itself, but also one that will resurface later as children grapple with common denominators for addition and subtraction. It was pretty well guaranteed that Risa's students would see the dots grouped in a series of different arrays. Many other contexts (see Figures 7.2 and 7.3, for example) would likely generate similar discussions. Using the array in Figure 7.2, a teacher might ask questions similar to those Risa did, but here the number and groupings of the dots point up relationships between ¼, ⅛, ⁸⁄₃₂, ¼ of 32, ⅛ of 32, etc. With the money context in Figure 7.3, students are likely to talk about fractions and their decimal equivalents.

Let's return to Joel Spengler's sixth-grade classroom and observe a minilesson based on a string of previously prepared problems for adding fractions. Joel is using a clock model to encourage students to use the strategy of *finding a familiar, landmark whole*—in this case one hour.

"I live on the Upper West Side of Manhattan, near Central Park," Joel begins, "and I've been thinking that I should make use of the park and start exercising. I was talking about this earlier with my friend Alex, and he said

FIGURE 7.2

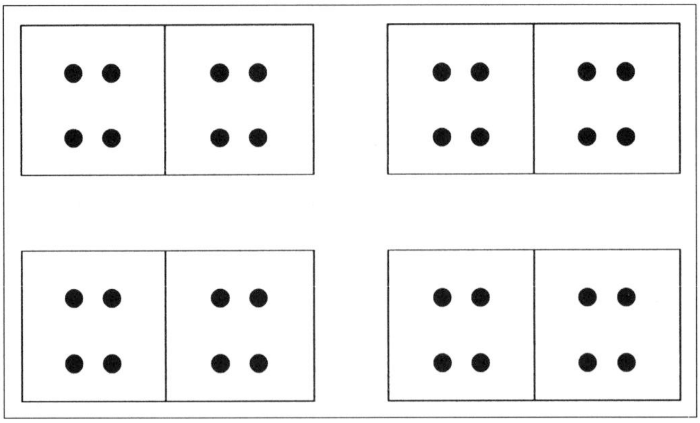

that I should start by running for one third of an hour and then walk for one fourth of an hour. How much time is that altogether?"

"Thirty-five minutes," Max answers quickly.

"How did you figure that?" Joel asks.

"Well, one third of an hour is twenty minutes, and one fourth of an hour is fifteen minutes. So that's thirty-five minutes."

Joel draws a clock on the chalkboard, marking the twenty minutes and the fifteen. "You just knew that one third of an hour was twenty minutes. What if one didn't know that? Could we prove it? Veronica?"

"There's sixty minutes in an hour. One third of sixty is twenty, and one fourth of sixty is fifteen."

"Okay, does everybody agree with that?" When everyone nods in agreement, Joel asks, "And so what portion of an hour is the thirty-five minutes?"

"Thirty-five sixtieths," Veronica replies quickly.

"It could also be seven twelfths," Lucy joins in. "You could think of it in five-minute chunks."

Joel adds the five-minute chunks to the drawing (see Figure 7.4) and writes $\frac{1}{3} + \frac{1}{4} = \frac{20}{60} + \frac{15}{60} = \frac{35}{60} = \frac{7}{12}$. Then he continues with his string. "Another friend of mine, Jesse, said I should push myself more and run for half an hour and then walk for two thirds of an hour." Joel writes the problem $\frac{1}{2} + \frac{2}{3}$ as he talks. "How much is that? Victor?"

"One hour and ten minutes—seventy minutes." Victor has the answer quickly, as do most of the other children.

"How did you think about it?"

"I thought of the half as thirty minutes," Victor explains, and Joel writes $\frac{1}{2} = \frac{30}{60}$. "Then I thought of the two thirds as forty minutes." Joel writes $\frac{2}{3} = \frac{40}{60}$. "So thirty plus thirty made an hour and I had ten minutes left."

FIGURE 7.3

"That's interesting," Joel comments, writing $^{30}\!/_{60} + ^{10}\!/_{60}$ under the $^{40}\!/_{60}$, "and what portion of an hour was that?"

Veronica responds, "The thirty sixtieths is equal to one half, so two thirds is equal to ten sixtieths plus one half, or forty sixtieths."

Chloe attempts to offer another strategy, but becomes confused. "I knew that ten sixtieths was ten minutes, too, so then I added three sixtieths to that."

"So did you get thirteen sixtieths?" asks Joel.

"No—no—I mean—one sixtieth?"

Joel focuses on the context to help her realize what she is trying to do. "Are you saying that ten minutes is one sixtieth of an hour?"

"Oh, no—I mean ten minutes is one sixth of an hour, and the half hour is three sixths, so that's four sixths." She clarifies her thinking for herself as she explains, and Joel marks the ten-minute chunks on the model of the clock as she talks it through. She seems clear, as do the other children, so he goes on with his string.

"Okay, so what if I run for one third of an hour, walk for twenty-five minutes, and then get a second wind and run for another quarter of an hour?" As he talks he writes $^{1}\!/_{3} + ^{25}\!/_{60} + ^{1}\!/_{4}$.

"It's one hour; it's twenty plus twenty-five plus fifteen. Sixty minutes." Everyone agrees with Veronica's explanation, and Joel writes $^{20}\!/_{60} + ^{25}\!/_{60} + ^{15}\!/_{60} = ^{60}\!/_{60} = 1$.

Although Joel has thought about the problems beforehand and has a string of related problems ready, he does not put all the problems on the board at once. Instead he writes one at a time, and children discuss their strategies before the subsequent problem is presented. This way, the children can consider the strategies from the prior problem as well as the numbers, and they are prompted to think about the relationships of the problems in the string as they go along. Sometimes, depending on the strategies

FIGURE 7.4
Clock Model

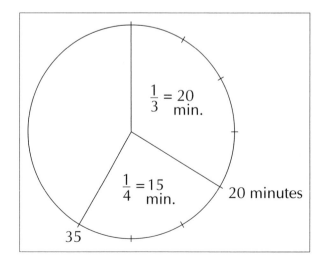

he hears, Joel adjusts the problems in his planned string on the spot to ensure that the strategies he is attempting to develop are discussed and tried out. Let's watch him in action.

"Let's go back to one half plus one sixth for a minute. Chloe, earlier you said we could think of this as forty sixtieths, or four sixths, right? And, Lucy, you suggested we could also think of the clock in five-minute chunks. Could we use that here? Turn to the person you're sitting next to and discuss this." Joel wants the students to think about a variety of common denominators.

After giving the students a brief time to discuss how twelfths could be used and ensuring that everyone seems clear, Joel has Lucy share, and he writes $\frac{2}{12} + \frac{6}{12} = \frac{8}{12}$. Once again he uses the clock model, indicating the five-minute chunks. He now has this string of equations on the board: $\frac{40}{60} = \frac{2}{3} = \frac{4}{6} = \frac{3}{6} + \frac{1}{6} = \frac{1}{2} + \frac{1}{6} = \frac{2}{12} + \frac{6}{12} = \frac{8}{12}$. But he wants his students to consider further factors and multiples, so he asks, "We've been using a clock model to help us add fractions today. What made that a helpful model with these problems? Would this model be helpful with all numbers? For example, adding sevenths? Turn to the person you're next to and talk about this."

After allowing a few minutes for discussion and reflection, Joel starts another whole-group discussion. As a class they generate a list of fractions for which the clock model is helpful: twelfths, thirds, sixths, sixtieths, and fourths. They discuss why and then Joel concludes his minilesson with a suggestion that in the future when they are adding or subtracting these fractions, they might want to picture a clock and use it as a mental tool.

Choosing a Common Whole

Another day Joel uses the double number line to develop addition strategies.

"Let's start math workshop today with some work on addition," Joel begins. He writes $\frac{1}{4} + \frac{1}{5}$ on the chalkboard. "Is there a number we could use for say . . . an imaginary bike trip, that might help us calculate this problem? Hamilton?"

"One hundred," Hamilton is quick to respond.

"Okay. So I'll draw a line to represent the track and I'll write the one hundred miles at the end. How does this help? What did you do next?"

"I thought of it like percentages . . . out of one hundred," Hamilton explains. "Four times twenty-five is one hundred, and five times 20 is one hundred . . . so you just add up the twenty-five and the twenty . . . that's forty-five out of one hundred."

On the board, Joel represents his thinking on a double number line (see Figure 7.5) commenting as he draws, "So let me represent your strategy on the track. You knew one fourth of the trip was 25 miles, and one fifth of the trip was twenty miles. So how much of the trip have I done?

"Forty-five miles."

"Out of the one hundred, right?" Joel asks for clarification and then adds 45 to the bottom of the line, and the fraction, $\frac{45}{100}$, to the top of the line. Does everyone agree with Hamilton?"

Most acknowledge agreement, but Jeremy has his hand raised. "Jeremy, you have a comment?"

"Yes. I agree with Hamilton, but I did it a different way."

"How did you do it?

"I made the track twenty miles," Jeremy explains. Joel draws a new line and labels it *20* as Jeremy continues explaining, "I knew you had to do five times four because that is twenty. So one quarter of twenty is five."

Another classmate, Elise, interrupts. "I have a question first." She turns to Hamilton. "Why did you choose one hundred? Why not fifty . . . or whatever . . . ?"

"Because I was thinking about percentages."

"And so that made it easy for you?" Joel asks.

Hamilton nods, and Joel continues, "But now we'll try twenty. Alexis, you look like you want to finish the strategy that Jeremy was sharing." Joel tries to bring more voices into the conversation.

Alexis smiles, and explains, "One quarter of twenty is five and one fifth of twenty is four." Joel draws the double number line representation (see Figure 7.6) and Alexis continues, "So that's nine."

"Could I also write nine twentieths here?" Joel inquires pointing to where he has written $\frac{1}{4} + \frac{1}{5} = \frac{45}{100} = \frac{9}{20}$.

"Yes, because they are equivalent," Alexis offers. Several other classmates nod to show their agreement.

Joel pushes further. "Could we prove that?"

"It's like one track is five times as big," Hamilton offers. "Twenty times five is one hundred and nine times five is forty-five."

"Nice way of thinking about it," Joel comments and points out how he has multiplied the numerator by five, and the denominator by five. "Let's try

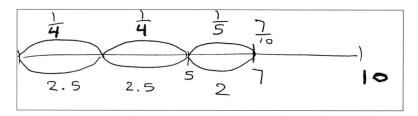

FIGURE 7.5   *Joel's Double Number Line Representing Hamilton's Strategy*

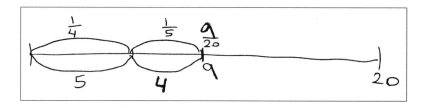

FIGURE 7.6   *Joel's Double Number Line Representing Jeremy's Strategy*

another problem and use this track idea again." Joel writes $\frac{2}{4} + \frac{1}{5}$ and continues to try to bring more children into the discussion. "Walker, do you have a good number for this one?"

"One hundred," Walker responds quickly. "Because I think of quarters. One quarter is twenty-five, but it's two quarters so that is fifty. One fifth is twenty."

"So what fraction of the course is it?" Joel asks for his final answer.

"Seventy hundredths, or seven tenths."

Joel writes $\frac{70}{100} = \frac{7}{10}$ and queries, "These are equivalent?"

Walker agrees, but Joel continues exploring the equivalence on the double number line, "Okay, then let's look at this as if the track is ten miles and see. How much is the one fourth?" he asks as he draws the line (see Figure 7.7).

At first, there is puzzlement, but then Hamilton responds, "Oh. Two and a half miles."

"So another fourth gets us to five out of the ten miles. And the fifth?" Joel records the result in miles underneath the line and the fractions above the line as he talks. "So the total miles is seven. And so the fraction is seven tenths?"

"Yes, but it almost seems like cheating. It's too easy. The seven and the ten are already there underneath the line," Hamilton says with a laugh.

Joel laughs back good-naturedly. "That's the point! We can make fraction problems friendly like this. It's like turning the fractions into friendly numbers so that we can do the computation mentally. We have two lines here that we can compare simultaneously, what's on top, and what's underneath. The top has the fractions. On the bottom we have the miles."

Whereas the clock model is limited to certain fractions, the double number line is an open model—any common denominator can be chosen and used. Initially the double number line is a model of the students' thinking, a representation Joel uses to enable everyone to visualize and discuss various strategies that come up. But as the students become more and more comfortable with it, it becomes a mental model—a tool to think with.

Multiplying Numerators and Denominators

The open array is a powerful support when multiplying and dividing fractions. In the following scenario, Maarten Dolk uses it with a group of inservice teachers.

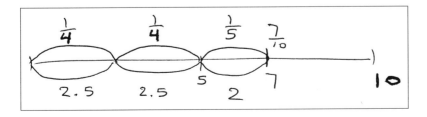

FIGURE 7.7 $\frac{2}{4} + \frac{1}{5}$

Maarten writes $\frac{1}{3} \times \frac{1}{4}$. Everyone quickly has an answer of $\frac{1}{12}$, and Maarten draws the open array in Figure 7.8a. Next he writes the problem $\frac{2}{3} \times \frac{1}{4}$.

"Well, that's just double the last one!" Marcia exclaims, noticing the relationships between the numbers Maarten is playing with.

"Tell us how you know that, Marcia."

"Because two thirds equals two times one third. So the answer has to be double."

Maarten draws the array in Figure 7.8b to represent her thinking and asks the group if they agree. When everyone does, Maarten writes the next problem: $\frac{2}{3} \times \frac{3}{4}$.

"Oh, so now it is just three times the last one!" Peter recognizes the relationship in Maarten's string.

"Why?" Maarten asks.

"Because three fourths is three times one fourth." Once again Maarten adds to the array (see Figure 7.8c).

"Or another way you could think about it," Cleo offers, "is as two times three times one twelfth. You could use the first problem to build from instead of the second. So now it is six times one twelfth."

"Oh, my gosh, that's why the algorithm works!" Sandy exclaims. "I'm embarrassed to say, but I just memorized the procedure. I never knew why."

"So what are you noticing now? Can you use the array to tell us what you mean?" Maarten asks for more clarification; he wants to see whether she can relate the algorithm to the arrays he has drawn.

Sandy takes a moment to think, then comes to the chart and points to the first array. "This square is one twelfth. When you look at the last array,

FIGURE 7.8a
$\frac{1}{3} \times \frac{1}{4} = \frac{1}{12}$

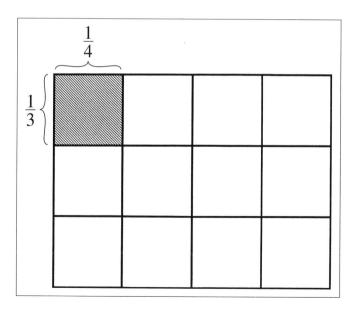

you see that the numerators form a two-by-three array—so now it's six times one twelfth."

"Oh, that's cool, Sandy," Marcia says. "It's also like the numerators form the inside array, and the denominators form the outside, larger one. So you can just multiply the numerators and multiply the denominators."

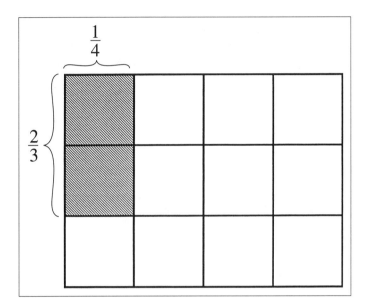

FIGURE 7.8b
$\frac{2}{3} \times \frac{1}{4} = \frac{2}{12}$

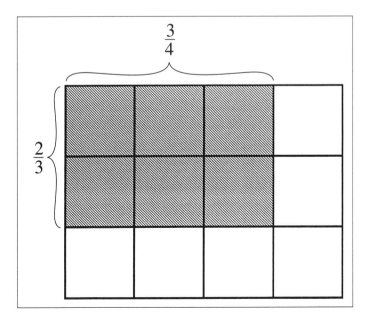

FIGURE 7.8c
$\frac{2}{3} \times \frac{3}{4} = \frac{6}{12}$

"What if the problem had been three halves times four thirds?" Maarten pushes.

Marcia pauses for a moment but then responds, "Oh, neat, now the numerators are the bigger array and the array made by the denominators is in the inside. And you can see how it fits inside twice!"

Maarten draws the open array to represent her thinking (see Figure 7.9), gives everyone a few moments to think about what Sandy and Marcia have said, and then comments, "Okay, so this time I'll put up two problems, instead of one. You make the open arrays to show how they are related, then turn to the person you are sitting next to and share your drawings." Maarten writes $\frac{1}{3} \times \frac{1}{7}$, then $\frac{3}{5} \times \frac{4}{7}$. As the class members work, Maarten moves around, looks at their drawings, and listens to their conversations.

Swapping Numerators and Denominators

Ensured that everyone seems to understand the ideas discussed thus far, he puts up the next problem in his string, $\frac{4}{5} \times \frac{3}{7}$.

"Oh, wow! It's the same thing!" Carla is intrigued. "Does that mean you can always swap the numerators when you're multiplying fractions?"

"Or you could swap the denominators!" Peter exclaims.

"Why?" Maarten asks. "Turn to the person you are next to and talk about this."

Cleo and Roger are sitting next to each other. Maarten listens in on their conversation. Cleo is trying to convince Roger, who is still not sure it will always work. "It has to be so. The problem is really three times four times

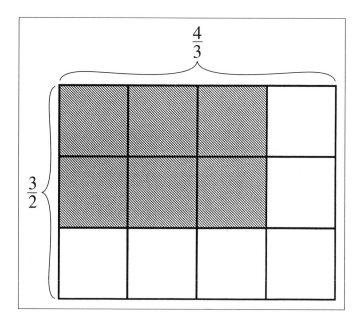

FIGURE 7.9
$\frac{3}{2} \times \frac{4}{3} = \frac{12}{6}$
The Whole Is Six

one fifth times one seventh. Because of the associative property you can multiply whatever pieces you want first. You can associate them any way you want. It could be four times one fifth times three times one seventh or four times one seventh times three times one fifth, whatever you want."

Roger is still puzzled. I need to see it in the array." He begins to draw an array for $\frac{3}{5} \times \frac{4}{7}$ (see Figure 7.10a). "Okay, I understand this. It's a three by four inside a five by seven. So that is twelve thirty-fifths. Now I'll draw the other problem, four fifths times three sevenths." This time he draws the inside array as a four by three, but the outside array stays the same (see Figure 7.10b). "Oh, wow, look! The inside just turns ninety degrees, that's all. The relationship stays the same! So if we swapped the denominators—let's see—the outside array would just turn!"

When the whole-group discussion resumes, Maarten asks Roger to share what he and Cleo have been discussing. When he finishes, Sandy also has an insight she wants to share. "I see what you mean about the associative property being at play here. But I was also thinking that the commutative property is. One fifth times one seventh is one thirty-fifth. And that is also true if it is one seventh times one fifth. Since the numerators can also be swapped, it's either three times four or four times three. But either way it's twelve times one thirty-fifth—or twelve squares out of the thirty-five." She points to Roger's arrays. "Swapping *is* the commutative property. That's what it means—to *commute*."

"These would have been the next problems in my string, but you're all way ahead of me." Maarten smiles, pleased with their thinking, as he writes the following problems: $\frac{3}{8} \times \frac{4}{9}$; $\frac{5}{6} \times \frac{3}{5}$; and $\frac{1}{3} \times \frac{5}{8}$. "Let's see if we can figure out when this swapping strategy might be helpful."

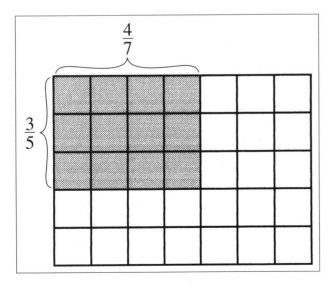

FIGURE 7.10a
$\frac{3}{5} \times \frac{4}{7} = \frac{12}{35}$

"Wow, cool." With oohs and ahs the group quickly transforms the problems into simple ones: $\frac{3}{8} \times \frac{4}{6} = \frac{4}{8} \times \frac{3}{6} = \frac{1}{2} \times \frac{1}{3}$; $\frac{5}{6} \times \frac{2}{5} = \frac{2}{6} \times 1$; $\frac{4}{5} \times \frac{5}{8} = 1 \times \frac{1}{2}$.

These teachers have of course constructed ideas relative to swapping and the multiplication algorithm much faster and more smoothly than middle school children will. The open array and strings Maarten used, however (the string in its entirety is shown in Figure 7.11), can be very helpful for children as well. Maarten chose the numbers in his string carefully: each problem is related to the one before it and to the strategies he wants to discuss.

Getting Rid of the Fraction

The algorithm (multiplying numerators and denominators) and swapping are two important strategies for multiplying fractions. A third, *getting rid of the fraction,* is just as powerful. For example, if one wants to multiply $3\frac{1}{2} \times 18$, one can double the $3\frac{1}{2}$ to get rid of the fraction. If this amount is doubled, then the 18 needs to be halved. So now the problem is 7×9, one that is easily solved mentally. If the original problem was $3\frac{1}{4} \times 28$, we could get rid of the fraction by multiplying the $3\frac{1}{4}$ by 4. This gives 13. If we now take $\frac{1}{4}$ of 28 we get 7. So now the problem is 13×7. Once again we can solve it mentally. Try $3\frac{1}{5} \times 50$; the problem can be turned into 16×10!

To help children develop this strategy, just build a string of related problems (see Figure 7.12) in which several pairs of problems have the same answer. Children will quickly become intrigued with why the same answer occurs and a rich conversation and/or investigation is likely to ensue.

Getting rid of the fraction can also be helpful when dividing fractions. For example, if the divisor becomes one, the problem is solved! Take $3\frac{1}{3} \div \frac{1}{2}$. To get rid of the $\frac{1}{2}$ and make 1 we have to double it. With division we

FIGURE 7.10b
$\frac{3}{5} \times \frac{4}{7} = \frac{4}{5} \times \frac{3}{7} = \frac{12}{35}$

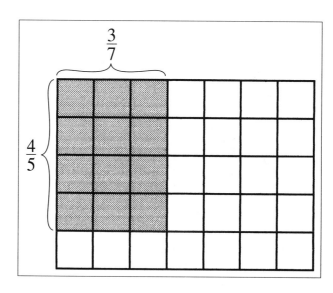

have to double the dividend, too, to keep the ratio constant. (Equivalent fractions, remember!) So now we have $6\frac{2}{3} \div 1$. Done! Or what if the problem had been $3\frac{1}{3} \div \frac{1}{3}$? Multiply both by 3, and now we have a very easy problem: $10 \div 1$! This idea, of course, is the basis of the invert-and-multiply algorithm. To make the divisor one, we can multiply by the reciprocal (in this case, $\frac{3}{1}$). Strings to explore this idea are shown in Figure 7.13. (Readers who feel lost here may want to refer to volume 2 of this series where we discuss

FIGURE 7.11
Maarten's String

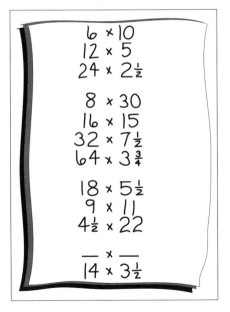

FIGURE 7.12
String in Which Several Pairs of Problems Have the Same Answer

FIGURE 7.13
*Strings to Explore
Multiply by the
Reciprocal*

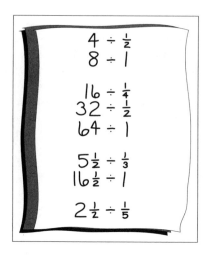

multiplication and division strategies in more depth, particularly the reducing strategy for division.)

Developing Strategies for Computation with Decimals

Volumes 1 (addition and subtraction) and 2 (multiplication and division) of this series discuss several strategies for the four operations with whole numbers. Because decimals are specific instances of fractions, and because they rely on our place value system, all these whole number strategies come into play. For example, compensation, a powerful mental math strategy for addition, can be used with decimals to make the problem friendly. Try adding 71.97 + 28.2. If we make the problem 71.17 + 29 by removing .8 from 71.97 and adding it to 28.2, we can get rid of one of the decimals—compensating in order to move to a landmark number. Or we could turn it into 72 + 28.17. Either way the problem has been made friendly enough to calculate mentally. Thinking about money also helps. One could think about adding 72 dollars and 28 dollars and then the difference of 17 cents. The open number line is very helpful here as a model to represent learners' thinking. (This is described in depth in volume 1.)

Using Money

Because money is such a powerful and ever present context in children's lives, it can be used to develop landmark numbers like .25, .50, and .75. Let's listen as Carol Mosesson's students discuss their multiplication strategies with decimals based on the use of money. Zenique is sharing how he came up with 1.80 as the answer to .20 × 9.

"Five twenty cents is one dollar," he begins, "so another four is eighty cents."

"Money is a clever way to think about that problem, Zenique." Carol writes .25 × 9 on the board. "How about this one? Shakira?"

"Three hundred—no, two-point-twenty-five. I counted by quarters."

"How many twenty-fives would it take to make three hundred?" Carol probes.

Shakira answers quickly, "Twelve."

Carol is surprised. "Wow, how did you know that so fast?"

"I knew four quarters made a dollar, so times three, that's twelve."

"That's exactly how I did it," Olana joins in. "I got two-point-twenty-five because I knew that four times twenty-five was a hundred, because that's like four quarters. So another four times twenty-five is another dollar. And one more quarter is two-point-twenty-five."

To develop this type of thinking, teachers can begin a minilesson using real coins, or pictures of coins, in an array. For example, if a four-by-four array of quarters is shown, many children will explain that they know that each row is a dollar. Because quarters are worth twenty-five cents, the problem can then be written as $16 \times .25$ and strategies developed—$16 \times .25 = 4 \times (4 \times .25)$, for example. After several minilessons based on money, children are able to use it as a context even when the numbers are "bare," as in strings.

Using Fractions and Decimals Interchangeably

Once children develop a sense of landmark fractions like $\frac{1}{2}$, $\frac{1}{4}$, and $\frac{3}{4}$ and know the decimal equivalents, using them interchangeably is a powerful strategy. For example, 75×80 can easily be solved by thinking of the problem as $\frac{3}{4} \times 80$. You only have to remember to compensate for the decimal in the answer (multiply 60 by 100, because you treated 75 as $\frac{75}{100}$).

Minilessons can be designed to develop this ability. If the problems in a string progress from fractions to decimals to whole numbers, children quickly see the resulting patterns. For example, a string like $\frac{1}{4} \times 80$, $.25 \times 80$, 25×80, $\frac{1}{2} \times 60$, $.5 \times 60$, $.50 \times 60$, $.50 \times .60$ produces the appropriate patterns in the answers, and children can use arrays to explore the relationships.

SUMMING UP . . .

When René Descartes said, "Each problem that I solved became a rule which served afterwards to solve other problems," he said it all. When children are given the chance to compute in their own ways, to play with relationships and operations, they see themselves as mathematicians and their understanding deepens. Such playing with numbers forms the basis for algebra and will take children a long way in being able to compute not only efficiently but elegantly. Max Dehn envisioned the power of mathematical play when he said: "Mathematics is the only instructional material that can be presented in an entirely undogmatic way." Why has it taken us so long to realize it?

8 | ASSESSMENT

If we do not change our direction, we are likely to end up where we are headed.
—*Chinese Proverb*

The previous chapters have documented a great deal of teaching and learning. They are filled with stories of middle school children and teachers hard at work: children, as they construct an understanding of fractions, decimals, and percents; teachers, as they grapple with ways to facilitate this journey. The learning is evident in the conversations we have overheard and in the children's work. But is there a more formal way to assess it? And what is assessment, anyway? Is it the same thing as documentation or evaluation? And most important, what is its purpose or function?

Over the last hundred years, answers to these questions have changed dramatically. For example, around the turn of the last century Sir Walter Alexander Raleigh wrote, "In an examination those who do not wish to know ask questions of those who cannot tell." Fifty years later, Bloom and Foskay wrote,

> There is one field in which a considerable sophistication has developed since 1920: the field of achievement testing. It is possible now to study the degree and nature of a student's understanding of school subjects with a subtlety not previously available. Modern objective achievement tests, when properly developed and interpreted, offer one of the most powerful tools available for educational research. Findings have been made through their uses that rise far above common sense. (p. 65; cited in van den Heuvel-Panhuizen, 1996)

In the fifties, sixties, and seventies, teaching and learning were seen as two separate processes. Teachers taught by transmission and feedback; learners practiced and studied. It was believed that the knowledge that resulted could be measured in terms of behavioral outcomes. Taxonomies of behavioral objectives were developed, and curricula were written to match the desired outcomes. (See the hierarchical taxonomies of Bloom et al. [1971] and Gagné [1965].) Content was broken down into skills and subskills, which were thought to accumulate into more encompassing concepts. Teachers were expected to focus all instruction toward these outcomes, and tests were de-signed to measure whether learners had "mastered" them (Bloom 1980).

The language used to discuss education during this period is interest-ing. *Skill* refers to skillful behavior, behavior that can be executed with skill. There is certainly skill involved in hammering nails or sawing wood. One can also type skillfully. But what do we mean when we talk about mathe-matical "skills"? Do skills constitute mathematical thinking, or did we begin to use that terminology because skills were outcomes that were easier to measure? Certainly, if proficiency with an algorithm is the goal, one can talk of skills. But do "skills" with performing algorithms really get to the heart of mathematical *thinking*?

The term *concept* is also grounded in behaviorism and the closely aligned psychology of associationism. One is said to have a concept of "fruit," for ex-ample, if it can be defined and associated with various exemplars—apples, peaches, etc. Back then, we assessed concepts by whether or not learners could associate exemplars—another easily measurable outcome. In mathe-matics, we typically used the term *concept* to refer to topics like place value or fractions. We measured outcomes by determining whether learners could associate a picture of ten bundled and two loose objects with the numeral 12, for example, or whether they wrote ⅗ when they saw three shaded parts out of a total of five. But is this term also a misnomer when one defines mathematics as mathematizing? Clearly, concepts do not equal big ideas, nor do skills equal strategies.

And *taxonomies,* by definition, categorize knowledge into a linear frame-work, not a landscape. Freudenthal objected to taxonomies because he saw them as a priori categories, postulated on logical grounds by designers of curricula, tests, and measurement tools (van den Heuvel-Panhuizen 1996). He argued that they were designed to categorize problems used in achieve-ment tests rather than to represent the genuine development of knowledge coming from a posteriori analysis of learners' work. To support his argument, he provided an example of how a taxonomy of outcomes that ascend in the order knowledge, recognition, application, integration, could actually be found in the reverse when one looks at it from the development of the learner:

> Let us follow the pattern using the knowledge of 3 < 4; this is in-tegrated by, for instance, comparing one's own family of three with the family of four next door; it is applied to other pairs of quanti-ties; it is recognized by means of a one-to-one relationship ("be-cause they have one more child"); and it becomes knowledge through the counting sequence 1, 2, 3, 4. . . . (cited in van den Heuvel-Panhuizen 1996, p. 22)

As outcomes became the focus, *what* we assessed and *how* we assessed it were determined by what was easy to assess and measure. By emphasizing the construction of the test items, it became easy to obtain a score and use this as a measure of evaluation. Assessment moved toward evaluation, be-cause with these so-called "objective, measurable outcomes" we now had the ability to compare learners with one another, teachers with one another, and schools with one another, or so we thought. The function of assessment became evaluation—both of the individual and the group. The tests provided teachers with little or no information that could inform their teaching. Although they now had a score for a learner on an achievement test, this score provided no insights into the learner's developing abilities, strategies, misconceptions, or ways of thinking. The scores were merely a quantitative way to compare learners with one another and to compare the number of correct answers with the total possible number of correct answers on a test. This ratio was assumed to be a score that reflected what students had learned.

Streefland (1981) has argued that assessment should be viewed not in the narrow sense of determining what the student has learned but from the standpoint of educational development—that it should provide teachers with information about what to teach. "Such reflective moments in education," he writes, "in which the teacher contemplates what has passed and what is still to come, are important" (p. 35; cited in van den Heuvel-Panhuizen 1996). But the direction in the sixties and seventies was away from such common sense, toward objective measurement (Bloom and Foskay 1967). And what a path this has led us down!

Assessment outcomes today not only define what will be taught but also are used as gates to educational programs and schools. They are used to determine how much federal money schools will get. They put teachers on the line for job security and promotion. They are even used to evaluate schools and districts, thus effecting property values and the demography of neighborhoods. They are a high-stakes game. And make no mistake about it, they drive instruction.

PERFORMANCE-BASED EVALUATION AND ASSESSMENT

In the eighties and nineties, frameworks for teaching and learning began to shift. Emphasis was placed on learning as a constructive activity rather than as the result of transmission, practice, and reinforcement. As this new view of learning took hold, the inadequacies of the prevailing methods of assessment became apparent. In the words of Freudenthal, "We know that it is more informative to observe a student during his mathematical activity than to grade his papers" (1973, p. 84; cited in van den Heuvel-Panhuizen 1996).

To meet the call for more "authentic" forms of assessment, tests were made up of open-ended tasks rather than closed questions with only one answer. These performance-based assessments were designed to evaluate students' activity, *how* they went about solving a problem, rather than their answers. For example, fifth graders might be asked to solve a problem like this one:

> A playground space is being designed. It will then be blacktopped and fenced. The amount of fencing that is available for the project is 1200 feet. Would it be better to fence a rectangular area that is

longer than it is wide, or a square area? Which would give a greater area to play in? Explain and show your thinking.

Notice two important aspects of this problem. First, there are no answers to choose from. Students must solve the problem in their own way. In that sense the problem is open. Second, students are asked to explain their thinking—to show their work and justify their answer. Opening up test items in such a way shifted assessment from isolated skills and concepts to something more holistic—mathematical activity in an authentic context. Responses were quantified by applying scoring rubrics.

This performance-based assessment, while a worthy attempt to analyze student thinking, brought with it a host of problems. First, a context meaningful in one culture may not be meaningful in another. (For an urban child, playground size depends on the space available, not the amount of fencing. In many rural areas playgrounds are not fenced in at all.) Second, many of the assessment problems were written in prose and therefore depended on the learner's reading ability. Then too, second-language issues and writing facility affected learners' abilities to explain and justify their thinking. Were we assessing mathematical activity or language, culture, and writing ability? Given that the predominant use of these assessments was still evaluation of students, teachers, and schools, this was a serious issue.

PORTFOLIO-BASED DOCUMENTATION

Some researchers (Pat Carini and Ted Chittendon, among others) stepped in and suggested that assessments focus on documentation of learning rather than evaluation. Portfolio assessment was one such alternative. Samples of children's work over time were placed in portfolios and used as evidence of children's capabilities. Teachers kept anecdotal records of their observations, interviewed their students, and wrote up their reflections. All materials were placed in the portfolio as evidence of the child's mathematical thinking. These portfolios obviously documented children's mathematical activity, but how did one describe and characterize the growth? Another set of questions arose. What made a good sample entry? What kind of rubric could be used to "score" a portfolio? Was there a way to standardize the outcomes so that they could be treated as objective measures—so that they could be used for evaluation? *Should* they be used for evaluation?

ASSESSING MATHEMATIZING

The shift to performance-based assessment and the use of portfolios was a change in direction toward assessing children's mathematizing, but rather than making the mathematizing visible, we seemed to be assessing how well children could explain their strategies. What does it mean to make mathematizing visible? What is the purpose of assessment when mathematics is defined as mathematizing?

Freudenthal argued that assessment should be meaningful and provide information that will benefit the connected act of teaching:

> Examining is a meaningful activity. The teacher should be able to check the influence of the teaching process, at least in order to know how to improve it. The student has the right to know whether he has really learned something. . . . Finally there are others who are interested in knowing what somebody has learned. (1973, p. 83; cited in van den Heuvel-Panhuizen 1996)

From this perspective, assessment needs to inform teaching. It needs "to foresee where and how one can anticipate that which is just coming into view in the distance" (Streefland 1985, p. 285). It needs to capture mathematizing, not the verbal prose explaining it. It needs to assess what the child can do, not what he can't do (De Lange 1992). It needs to capture where the child is on the landscape of learning—where she has been, what her struggles are, and where she is going. It must move from being static to being dynamic (van den Heuvel-Panhuizen 1996).

Assessment must be dynamic in the sense that it evaluates *movement*— the journey. But it must also be dynamic by being *directly connected to learning and teaching*. If we teach in a way that supports mathematizing, then assessment must do the same. The information gleaned in assessment should directly inform and facilitate adjustments in teaching. For assessment to capture genuine mathematizing, for it to become dynamic, several criteria must be in place (van den Heuvel-Panhuizen 1996):

1. Students' own mathematical activity must be captured on the paper.
2. The test items must be meaningful and linked to reality.
3. Several levels of mathematizing must be possible for each item.
4. Assessment should inform teaching.

Capturing Genuine Mathematizing

There is a difference between writing about how you solved a problem and having the work visible. If teachers are to capture actual work, they need to provide scrap paper as part of the test (van den Heuvel-Panhuizen 1996). Further, requiring students to use pens rather than pencils guarantees that all marks stay visible—nothing can be erased: different starts, changes in strategies, mistakes, rewriting, final figuring, all get captured. For example, note the three solutions in Figures 8.1, 8.2, and 8.3 for the problem, *Find two more multiplication problems with the same answer as* $\frac{4}{9} \times \frac{6}{8}$. The first child solves the problem mentally by swapping numerators; the other two use algorithms. The second child succeeds, but tediously. The third makes errors with the algorithm and worse, ends by concluding that $2 \times \frac{4}{9}$ is equivalent to $\frac{4}{9} \times \frac{6}{8}$. Comparing the visible mathematizing of these three children gives the teacher a lot of useable information about where they are in the landscape of learning and the landmarks and horizons each requires.

Even with bare computation problems, scrap paper can capture whether children multiply $.99 \times 46$ with an algorithm or whether they turn the problem into 46 by 1 and subtract .46, a strategy than can be done mentally. Scrap paper can also capture whether children solve 3½ × 14 by doubling and halving (turning it into 7 × 7) or whether they turn the 3½ into the decimal form 3.5 and laboriously use an algorithm.

Linking Contexts to Reality

Contexts must allow children to mathematize—they must be more than word problems camouflaging "school mathematics." They must be real or be able to be imagined by children, just as the investigations used in teaching must be. One way to do this is to use pictures or tell stories: see the submarine sandwiches problem in Figure 8.4.

Providing for Various Levels of Mathematizing

The assessment items must be open enough that children can solve them in many ways. In the past, the test items themselves became progressively more difficult. One of the main problems with this approach is that "the students' behavior respects neither the taxonomies of objectives, nor the a priori analysis of difficulties" (Bodin 1993, p. 123; cited in van den Heuvel-Panhuizen 1996). If we want to assess levels of mathematizing, then we need, instead, to open the tasks up and look at the *way* in which the answer to the question is found, not just *whether* the answer is found. For example, there are

FIGURE 8.1

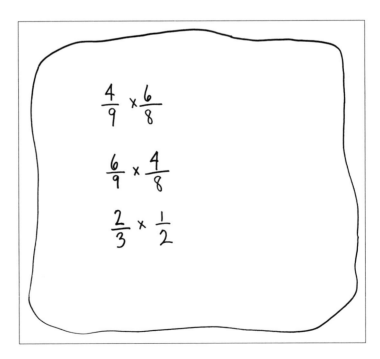

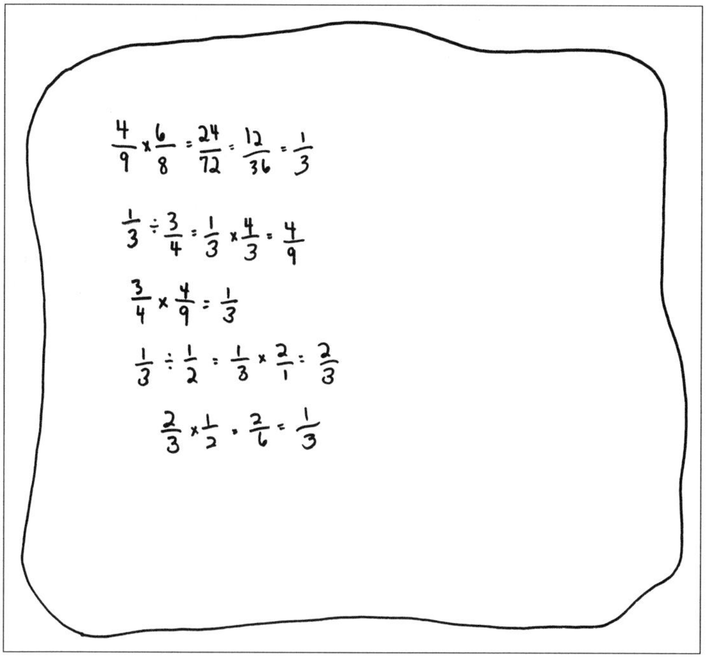

FIGURE 8.2

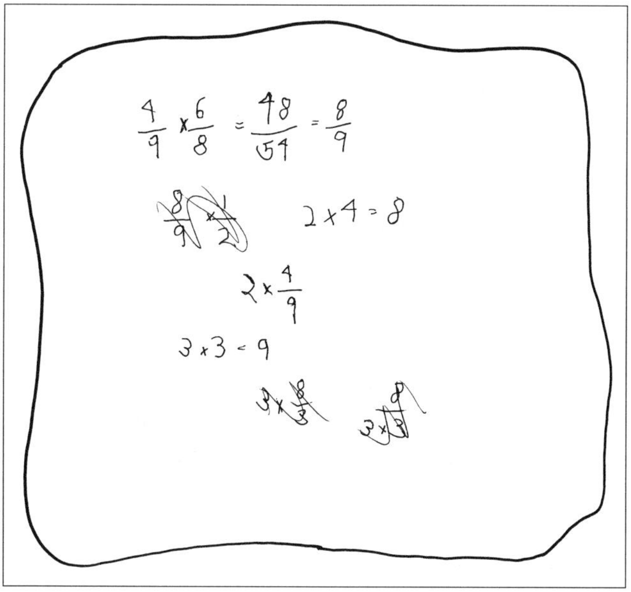

$$\frac{4}{9} \times \frac{6}{8} = \frac{24}{72} = \frac{12}{36} = \frac{1}{3}$$

$$\frac{1}{3} \div \frac{3}{4} = \frac{1}{3} \times \frac{4}{3} = \frac{4}{9}$$

$$\frac{3}{4} \times \frac{4}{9} = \frac{1}{3}$$

$$\frac{1}{3} \div \frac{1}{2} = \frac{1}{3} \times \frac{2}{1} = \frac{2}{3}$$

$$\frac{2}{3} \times \frac{1}{2} = \frac{2}{6} = \frac{1}{3}$$

FIGURE 8.3

$$\frac{4}{9} \times \frac{6}{8} = \frac{48}{54} = \frac{8}{9}$$

$$\frac{8}{9} \times \frac{1}{2} \qquad 2 \times 4 = 8$$

$$2 \times \frac{4}{9}$$

$$3 \times 3 = 9$$

$$3 \times \frac{8}{3} \qquad 3 \times \frac{8}{3}$$

many ways to solve the submarine sandwich problem in Figure 8.4. Children capable of a very high level of mathematizing would see it as a problem of 2 divided by 3 or 2 multiplied by ⅓. Others would need to cut up the subs to figure it out. Some would cut up the sandwiches into halves and then struggle with what to do with the half-sandwich remaining. When calculating the cost, some children might see it as ⅓ of $12 times 2 or ⅔ of $12, others might calculate it incorrectly as ⅔ of $24. Still others might proceed randomly trying to add various numbers to reach $24—a much lower level of mathematizing.

Informing Teaching

By assessing how a student mathematizes, teachers acquire information that enables them to determine how to proceed. They are able to understand where the child is within the landscape of learning. By analyzing the child's markings on the paper provided as part of the test, teachers are able to comprehend not only how the child is currently mathematizing but also what strategies she is trying out. The landscape of learning (which comprises strategies, big ideas, and models) informs the rubric used to analyze it but in turn also informs how it is taught. Because the landmarks become visible, teachers can determine appropriate horizons. In this way, learning and teaching are connected.

When the primary function of assessment is to inform teaching, evaluation is also redefined. Rather than "grading" schools and teachers with scores, we can characterize the mathematizing that is going on. We can evaluate the effect of various curricula and inservice professional development programs on this mathematizing. We can look at where the children are within the landscape of learning and describe the direction they need to go.

ASSESSMENT IN REFORMED CLASSROOMS

Assessing the Landscape of Learning

This book is built around a landscape of learning comprising the big ideas, strategies, and models related to fractions, decimals, and percents (see Figure 8.5). As teachers assess young mathematicians in the classroom, it is the landmarks the students pass (collectively and severally) in their journey through this landscape that informs teachers' questions, their instructional decisions, and the curriculum.

The landmarks in this journey are not necessarily sequential. Many paths can be taken toward this horizon. Some landmarks are, of course, precursors to others—repeated addition is a precursor to unitizing and the distributive property. On the other hand, some children will develop computation strategies that work, like doubling and halving, before fully understanding why they work—they try out a strategy and only later construct

Sharing subs

work area

Three children buy two giants subs.
The children share the subs fairly.

- How much of a sub does each child get? ....

A giant sub costs $12.-

- What should each child pay? ....

FIGURE 8.4

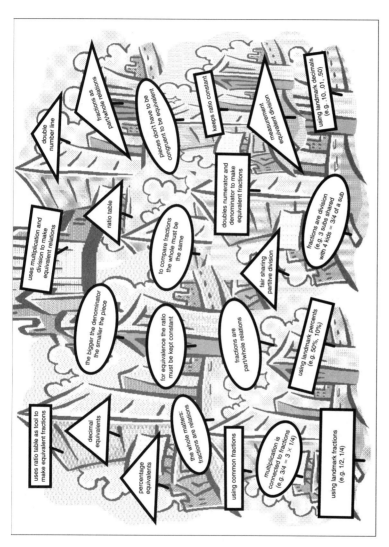

FIGURE 8.5   *The Landscape of Learning: Fractions, Decimals, and Percents on the Horizon Showing Landmark Strategies (Rectangles), Big Ideas (Ovals), and Models (Triangles)*

the big idea that explains the strategy. Others will construct the big idea first. Nor is this landscape definitive, or closed. Instead it represents what we have noticed so far in the journeys in our classrooms.

As in any real journey, new landmarks can appear, and new paths, uncharted before, can be carved out. This landscape is simply a representation of others' past journeys—it can inform teaching, but it can also be added to as teachers work with the young mathematicians in their classrooms. The landmarks are not a checklist or a list of behavioral outcomes. They are a means to focus on and describe students' mathematizing.

Assessing in the Moment

The best and perhaps most valid assessment happens while teaching and learning are taking place. As students interact in the classroom (with their teacher and with other students), as situations are explored and mathematized, teachers can observe the landmarks being passed. If teachers understand the landscape well, they become better able to observe, confer, and question in relation to important mathematical ideas, strategies, and models—to maximize mathematical teaching moments.

Anecdotal records document the journey, but they are also helpful reminders that can inform teaching. For example, let's look at this note jotted down by Barbara, a sixth-grade teacher, about Ana's work shown in Figure 8.6:

> I noticed today as I watched Ana at work that she flexibly used 3 different models to prove that ½ + ⅓ is not equivalent to ⅖. She used a clock model and a percent's equivalence, and she treated the fractions as numbers themselves when she argued that ½ even by itself is greater than ⅖. She also is able to add the fractions correctly with common denominators. Interestingly, though, she treated ⅓ as .33 when she used the decimal form, yet she said 33⅓% when working with percents. She did write the word "about" but does she realize that the numeral 3 continues in a repeating pattern? Does she understand that she could write .33⅓? Does she realize that $.\overline{33}$ is equivalent to ⅓—that it is a rational number? Does she realize the connection between percentages and decimals? Tomorrow I will ask the children to prove the decimal and percent equivalents to ⅓ and to hang them on a number line. I wonder what she will do?

Barbara's anecdotal records document what landmarks Ana has passed and where she might be going, what is on the horizon. And her notes will serve as a reminder to her that tomorrow she wants to encourage Ana to explore decimal and percentage connections, as well as repeating decimals as rational numbers on a number line—a very important idea underlying number theory. Her assessment is dynamic. It captures the flow of the journey

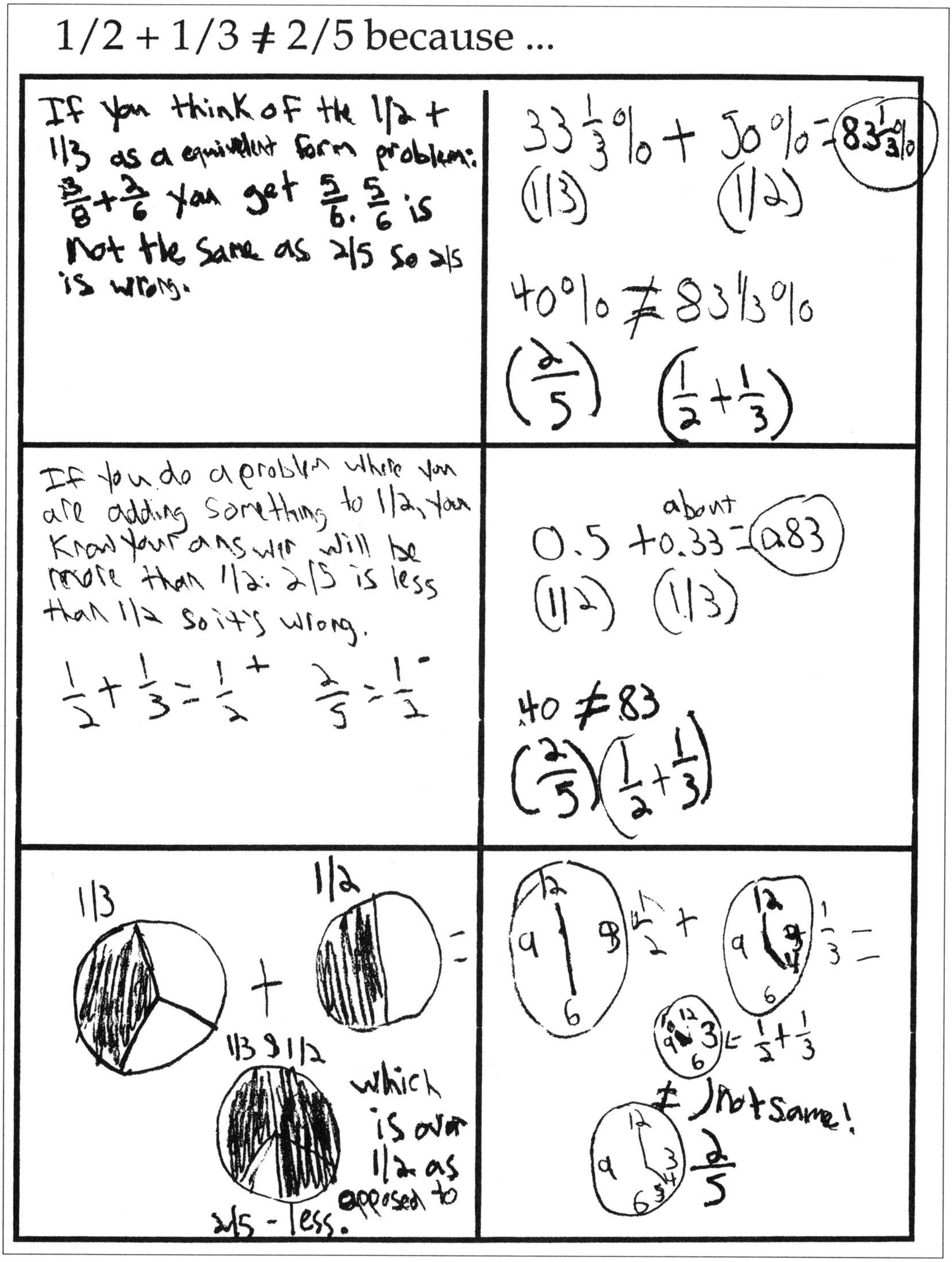

$1/2 + 1/3 \neq 2/5$ because ...

If you think of the $1/2 + 1/3$ as a equivalent form problem: $\frac{3}{6} + \frac{2}{6}$ you get $\frac{5}{6}$. $\frac{5}{6}$ is not the same as $2/5$ so $2/5$ is wrong.

$33\frac{1}{3}\% + 50\% = \boxed{83\frac{1}{3}\%}$

$(1/3) \quad (1/2)$

$40\% \neq 83\frac{1}{3}\%$

$\left(\dfrac{2}{5}\right) \quad \left(\dfrac{1}{2} + \dfrac{1}{3}\right)$

If you do a problem where you are adding something to $1/2$, you know your answer will be more than $1/2$. $2/5$ is less than $1/2$ so it's wrong.

$\dfrac{1}{2} + \dfrac{1}{3} = \dfrac{1}{2} + \qquad \dfrac{2}{5} = \dfrac{1}{2}^{-}$

about
$0.5 + 0.33 = \boxed{0.83}$

$(1/2) \quad (1/3)$

$.40 \neq .83$

$\left(\dfrac{2}{5}\right) \left(\dfrac{1}{2} + \dfrac{1}{3}\right)$

1/3   1/2

+   =

1/3 & 1/2

which is over 1/2 as opposed to 2/5 - less.

$\dfrac{1}{2} + \dfrac{1}{3} =$

$3 = \dfrac{1}{2} + \dfrac{1}{3}$

$\neq$)not same!

$\dfrac{2}{5}$

FIGURE 8.6

by documenting where Ana is on the landscape and what the journey will look like over the next few days.

Portfolio Assessment

Teachers can involve children in choosing and putting samples of work into a portfolio. Throughout the year, work can be dated and comments can be made in relation to the landscape. For example, Barbara might discuss Ana's piece of work with her. Together they might note how Ana was able to model fractions using a clock, percentages, and decimals. Over the next few days, as Ana further explores decimals and percents, she and Barbara will add more work to the portfolio. Over the course of the year, Ana's portfolio will become full of entries that serve as evidence of her mathematizing—and her development as a young mathematician.

Paper-and-Pencil Assessments

As long as the test items are designed in relation to the criteria described in this chapter, paper-and-pencil tests can provide important information for both students and teachers. For example, noting how Ana proved that $\frac{1}{2} + \frac{1}{3}$ was not equivalent to $\frac{2}{5}$ on her scrap paper helped her teacher see what relations she understands. Compare her work with Dan's in Figure 8.7. He adds $\frac{2}{6} + \frac{2}{4}$ and gets $\frac{2}{10}$, and then argues that this amount is only half of $\frac{2}{5}$. He makes equivalent fractions but does he have much of an understanding of the magnitude of fractions? The scrap paper provides evidence of where these two children are on the landscape.

ASSESSMENT RESULTS

Mathematizing vs. Traditional Instruction

How do children in classrooms like those depicted in this book compare with children in traditional classrooms, in which mathematics is taught as procedures? To look at this question, an assessment with items that were open enough to capture various levels of mathematizing (van den Heuvel-Panhuizen, et al. 1999) was given to third, fourth, and fifth graders in classrooms in which the Mathematics in the City program was being well implemented. The same assessment was given to third, fourth, and fifth graders in the same schools or district who had been taught algorithms and given little opportunity to mathematize. Responses were coded with a rubric that reflected the landscape of learning. (During the first five years of Mathematics in the City, we worked only in elementary classrooms. Thus our formal assessment only went through grade 5.)

Overall, the children's answers were not significantly different; however, their position within the landscape of learning differed remarkably (van den Heuvel-Panhuizen and Fosnot 2001). Children in classrooms in which number relationships and context were emphasized outperformed

1/2 + 1/3 ≠ 2/5 because ...

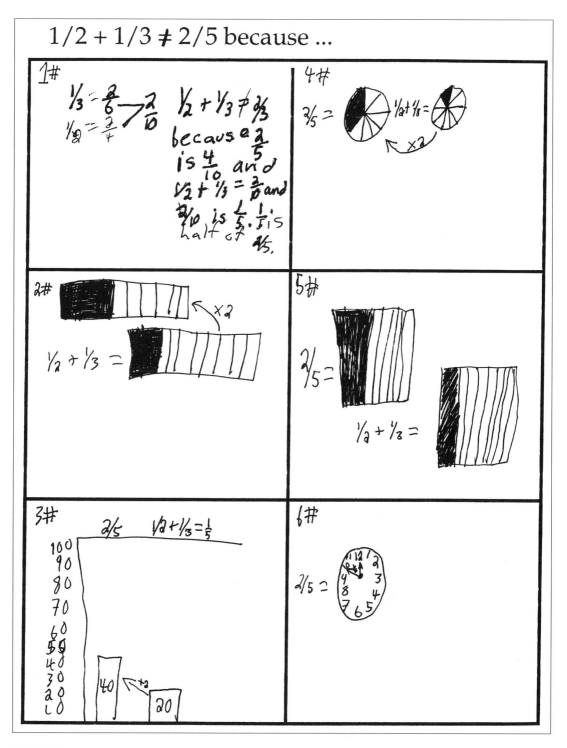

FIGURE 8.7

their traditionally taught peers significantly in using strategies representative of number sense. They easily composed and decomposed numbers to make them friendly, frequently computing mentally. Traditionally taught children relied on algorithms no matter what the numbers were. Children in reformed classrooms treated answers to problems within the context. For example, when asked to figure out how many half-dozen-size egg cartons would be needed to hold 800 golf balls, 20 percent of the children in the traditionally taught classrooms gave answers with remainders. None of the children in Mathematics in the City classrooms did.

Standardized Tests

Unfortunately most school districts are still held accountable on state and city standardized tests. In New York City, this test is the Terra Nova. It is a multiple-choice standardized achievement test similar to those used by most school districts. We again compared third, fourth, and fifth graders based on the results of this test and found a difference significant at the .0001 level (Fosnot, et al. 2001). The fourth-grade test results were of particular interest because this test is designed by the State and it produces a proficiency level statistic. The mean score of Mathematics in the City children fell in the middle of level three, the level considered proficient by New York State. The mean of the traditionally taught students fell within level two, a level below proficiency. Also, item analysis of the fifth-grade tests showed Mathematics in the City students to rate significantly higher on number understanding, geometry, measurement, data, and problem solving. (The difference on computation was not significant, although the mean score of Mathematics in the City children was higher.)

We share these results not because we believe standardized tests are the best way to assess learning. We don't, and we have tried to make that clear in this chapter. It is often argued, however, that change cannot occur in light of the pressure brought to bear because standardized assessments are used. Many districts mandate that teachers teach to the test. Pacing calendars aligned with the standardized tests determine curriculum in these districts, and direct instruction, practice, and test preparation characterize these classrooms. When this happens, assessment drives instruction and children are taught only the kind of thinking that can easily be assessed by these tests. They are not taught to think, to mathematize. Our data are proof that the practice of teaching to the test is a misappropriation of time. If children are taught in a way that allows them to construct understanding, they will perform better, even on standardized tests.

SUMMING UP . . .

The Chinese proverb used as the epigraph to this chapter states, "If we do not change our direction, we are likely to end up where we are headed." If we teach directly to standardized achievement tests, we may end up with children who can pass them but who know little mathematics. If we want to encourage mathematizing and the development of number relationships, we need to teach in a way that supports it.

Models of learning based on behaviorism and the belief that tests could measure this learning objectively drove early attempts at assessment. As our concept of learning shifted to include a deeper understanding of cognitive development, one characterized by constructivism, these tests were seen as insufficient. Performance-based assessment and portfolios replaced earlier tests. Problems arose, however, over whether we were assessing language or mathematics and how to quantify scores on portfolios.

Assessments need to inform teaching, and they need to reflect mathematizing. If assessments are developed that make mathematizing visible and include realistic items that can be mathematized on many levels, they can be beneficial. They can document the journey dynamically and depict where learners are on the landscape. The landscape of learning can serve as a framework, since it depicts important landmarks. However, it should not be seen as a list of outcomes but as a representation of many children's past journeys.

When young mathematicians are hard at work, they are thinking, they become puzzled, they become intrigued: they are learning to see their world through a mathematical lens. Assessment needs to capture the learning this lens reveals.

9 | TEACHERS AS MATHEMATICIANS

Life is good for only two things, discovering mathematics and teaching mathematics.

—*Siméon Poisson*

I'm sorry to say that the subject I most disliked was mathematics. I have thought about it. I think the reason was that mathematics leaves no room for argument. If you made a mistake, that was all there was to it.

—*Malcolm X*

Mathematics has beauties of its own—a symmetry and proportion in its results, a lack of superfluity, an exact adaptation of means to ends, which is exceedingly remarkable and to be found only in the works of the greatest beauty. When this subject is properly . . . presented, the mental emotion should be that of enjoyment of beauty, not that of repulsion from the ugly and the unpleasant.

—*J. W. A. Young*

TEACHER PREPARATION

So far this book has focused on *young* mathematicians at work—children between the ages of nine and thirteen hard at work constructing, questioning, mathematizing, and communicating their world through a mathematical lens. But if teachers are to be able to facilitate mathematical journeys for the learners with whom they work, they too need to have a strong understanding of the subject.

To this end, teacher education programs in the United States have added more and more mathematics courses. Over the last ten years there has been an impetus to make a liberal arts undergraduate degree a requirement for certification. Usually this has meant that education programs have been reduced to a single year (thirty credits) so that a bachelor of arts degree can still be obtained in four years or a master of arts in five. In essence, the trend has been to increase the length of the overall program, increase the number of liberal arts courses, and decrease the number of education courses. Today, teachers in the United States are required to take more college mathematics courses than ever before, yet the gap between the needed and the actual content understanding seems to be widening. The cry for professional development has now become a roar. Why are our teachers so ill prepared?

Some critics blame the teachers. They push for stricter entrance requirements for teacher education programs—higher grade-point averages and better scores on entrance examinations. Many states have developed their own examinations and introduced tiered certifications—initial, provisional, permanent, professional. A master's degree is often necessary in order to receive a permanent license, and salaries have been raised. All of these reforms have produced little real change in teachers' competence in mathematics.

In the Netherlands a different tack has been taken. People who want to become primary school teachers in the Netherlands do not attend a university, pursue a liberal arts degree, or take courses in a mathematics department. Instead, they attend *Hogeschool,* a four-year post–high school program specifically focused on teacher preparation. During the four years, students take seven or eight courses in mathematics education, courses geared toward a deep understanding of the mathematical topics *they will be teaching.* Prospective teachers learn about the big ideas embedded in the topics, about how children's strategies develop, about important mathematical models. They learn about the role of context and how to use didactical models like the double number line and the open array. They explore number patterns and mental math strategies. They become strong mathematical thinkers *in relation to the topics they will be teaching*—the landscape they will travel through with their children. But is even this enough?

Korthagen and Kessel (1999) have argued that a major problem with teacher education programs is that they are grounded in theory and methods, in *episteme,* and what is taught does not transfer to the classroom. Prospective teachers have preconceptions about learning and teaching that come from their past experiences as students. These preconceptions are so strong they prove resistant to new learning, particularly when the new learning is divorced from practice. It's true that most teacher decision making is split second and grounded in perception, feelings, interpretation, and reaction (Dolk 1997). Teachers respond based on their subconscious beliefs about teaching and learning and on their overall vision of practice—beliefs and a vision developed during many years of being learners themselves, most often in classrooms in which mathematics was defined as a discipline to be transmitted.

Teachers who are already in the classroom are rarely different. Although they have more experience, their belief systems are often not aligned with the belief systems implicit in the new curricula or in education reform. John is typical. Asked about his beliefs about teaching he says, "How do I view the process of teaching? Part actor, part salesman. You have this body of knowledge that you have to get across to kids, but most students really don't want to be in school, so you have to sell them on this education kick. If you don't make your presentation good and you're not a good actor, they're not going to buy" (Fosnot 1993). Unless these beliefs are challenged and modified, when John is given new curricula based on constructivism, he will assume that the purpose of problem solving is to motivate children. He will see activity as important to promote interest. He will adapt new pedagogical strategies, but he will see them as new strategies to help him "get the body of knowledge across." He will confuse constructivist-based practice with discovery learning.

How do we help teachers (both preservice and inservice) develop a new conception of the nature of mathematics, one based on the human activity of making meaning through a mathematical lens? How do we help them revise the picture of what should be happening in the classroom? These two questions get at the heart of what is required in teacher education if reform is to be successful. Providing teachers with new textbooks or new pedagogical strategies will produce only superficial changes. The new strategies will be implemented within the constructs of the belief systems teachers already hold.

To get John and teachers like him to analyze and reflect on their beliefs, teacher education itself must undergo radical change. It needs to be grounded in new visions of practice based on how students learn. This often means creating disequilibrium with regard to prior conceptions. Rather than basing our work with teachers on *episteme*, we need to look to a framework based on *phronesis* and *constructivism* (Fosnot 1989, 1993, 1996; Korthagen and Kessel 1999). *Phronesis* is situation-specific knowledge related to the context in which it is used—in this case, the process of teaching and learning. Constructivism describes learning as the process of building one's own understanding by modifying prior schemes and structures. Rather than teaching teachers about theory, which we then expect them to apply, we need to give them experiences that involve action, reflection, and conversation within the context of teaching and learning. They need to construct new beliefs, new visions of what it means to teach and learn mathematics. They need to experience an environment in which mathematics is taught as mathematizing and learning is seen as constructing.

When teachers themselves model situations mathematically, construct solutions, set up relationships, and defend their ideas to their peers, their visions of mathematics pedagogy and their definitions of mathematics begin to shift. By reflecting on their own learning and what facilitated it, they begin to form new beliefs—ones that often contradict prior beliefs. These beliefs in turn will become the basis for the way in which they react, question, and interact during learning/teaching moments. Teachers also need more situation-specific knowledge that can inform their decision making—more knowledge about how children develop mathematical ideas and strategies, a better ability to see and understand the mathematics in children's work. They need to understand mathematics as the human activity of mathematizing. And they need to understand the landscape of learning.

Throughout this book we have provided illustrations of teachers who define mathematics as mathematizing, who value their students' mathematical ideas and strategies, who promote genuine mathematical discourse within a community of mathematicians. These teachers walk the edge between the structure of mathematics and student development, between the individual and the community. In fact, they are willing to *live* on the edge, not always knowing the direction the path will take—to challenge themselves mathematically. They have acquired an in-depth understanding of the mathematical topics they teach and of the landscape of learning—the big ideas, the strategies, and the models. But they have done more. They have come to see themselves as mathematicians, to understand that mathematics is the human activity of mathematizing. They have come to see the beauty and joy in creating. As the mathematician J. B. Shaw once wrote, "The mathematician is fascinated with the marvelous beauty of the forms he constructs, and in their beauty he finds everlasting truth" (cited in Rose 1988). These teachers have come to love mathematical inquiry, and they have learned to mathematize their world.

LEARNING TO MATHEMATIZE

Once again, the most vivid way to illustrate what we mean is to have you listen in during a Mathematics in the City teacher education session as the participants grapple with some mathematical ideas and then reflect on their learning and teaching.

Exploring the Edge

Cathy Fosnot and Willem Uittenbogaard, the instructors, have asked the participants (all Pre-K–8 teachers) to explore various fractions, decimals, and percents (see Figure 9.1) and to determine where they should each go on a number line, literally a clothesline stretched across the room.

Although on the surface this may appear to be a simple equivalence activity, devoid of context, it is much more difficult and richer. The quantities chosen are related in interesting ways, as the subsequent dialogue will show. Also, the fractions, decimals, and percents are being treated as rational numbers: investigating them as quantities and placing them on the number line—actually building a "number space"—*is* the context. Creating the number line brings measurement, magnitude, and relationships to the fore. The participants are learners in a mathematical environment—one where the number system is "under construction."

"There's a pattern—some of these are related," Barbara explains to the other three members of her group. "See, one half is easy, because it is halfway between zero and one. And we know that it is equal to zero-point-five and fifty percent. So one fourth is half of the distance between zero and one half, and since that is twenty-five percent, one eighth must be twelve-point-five percent."

"That's cool," says Pierre, another member of the group. "So one sixteenth would be equivalent to six-point-twenty-five percent, since that is one half of twelve-point-five percent. And one thirty-second is three-point-one-twenty-five percent. It's so easy when you think of relationships. It's embarrassing to admit but I never thought of fractions, decimals, and percents like this before. I was just taught how to calculate them."

"Don't be embarrassed," Lena says. She and Kate, the remaining two members of the group, laugh supportively. Lena continues, "Me, too! I was taught to set it up as an equivalent fraction like this," she writes $\frac{1}{16} = \frac{?}{100}$, "then to divide the sixteen into one hundred to get the percent. I mean, I guess I knew that worked because percents had to do with hundredths—but it was more like a rule to me, rather than a relationship."

PLACE THESE NUMBERS ON THE NUMBER LINE

75% $16\frac{2}{3}$%   2.6   0.363636 . . . $66\frac{2}{3}$% $\frac{1}{5}$ $\frac{1}{10}$

0.090909 . . . $\frac{2}{5}$ 0.571428571428 . . . $\frac{1}{3}$ 0.75

$\frac{4}{5}$ $\frac{1}{7}$ $\frac{1}{6}$ 0.125   0.999 . . .   15% $\frac{1}{2}$ $\frac{2}{3}$

$14\frac{2}{7}$%   5% $\frac{2}{15}$ 0.112123123412345 . . .   0.454545 . . .

0.1666 . . . $\frac{3}{8}$ $\frac{4}{11}$ 20%   0.66 $\frac{1}{5}$ $1\frac{1}{4}$

0.142857142857 . . . $\frac{5}{8}$ 0.41666 . . . $33\frac{1}{3}$% $\frac{4}{7}$

$\frac{5}{9}$ $44\frac{4}{9}$ 5.05   0.333 . . .   0.001   0.0833 . . .

1.333 . . . $\frac{5}{11}$ 1   0.8   75%   0.45 $\frac{4}{3}$ $5\frac{1}{2}$

FIGURE 9.1

Lena's admission that for her mathematics involved rules rather than relationships is something many teachers can identify with. Since their instruction was often in the form of procedures, practice, explanation, and application—rather than construction—many never saw mathematics as creative, as something you inquired about. Albert Einstein once wrote, "It is nothing short of a miracle that modern methods of instruction have not yet entirely strangled the holy curiosity of inquiry. . . . Everything that is really great and inspiring is created by the individual who can labor in freedom" (cited in Eves 1988). But for most teachers, traditional mathematics instruction *did* strangle mathematical inquiry. Many have done everything in their power to avoid mathematics courses, and a large percentage of these teachers suffer from what is commonly called "math anxiety." The first step in working with teachers is to dissipate their fears and to engage them with the fascination of playing with mathematical relationships.

At a nearby table another group is having a similar discussion, but they are working on sevenths. They explain their ideas to Cathy, who has joined them.

"We started with .142857142857. . . . To make the equivalent percent we just moved the decimal point to the right two places," explains Ina.

"I didn't go to that school," Cathy laughs. "Can you help me understand why that rule works?"

The group laughs too. They are familiar with Cathy's questions by now and know that she often uses that reply when someone suggests a rote procedure. It is her way of checking to see if understanding is there, too. This time it is. Ina explains that she is just multiplying by one hundred, since percentage means out of a hundred.

"Okay. So then how did you get the fraction equivalent?" Cathy asks.

"That puzzled us for a while," Ina admits.

Lucienne, sitting next to Ina and working with a handheld calculator, clarifies. "Right. First we tried dividing 142,857 by a million, because that is what .142857 means, but then we realized how stupid that was because we just got the decimal number back! Next we tried the .2857 part divided by ten thousand, but that was also stupid—the decimal point just moved again! Then Joanne suggested we set it up as an equivalent. See." She points to the equation shown in Figure 9.2. "So then we knew you had to cross-multiply!"

Cathy paraphrases to clarify, then smiles and begins, "I didn't—"

Everyone laughs and Lucienne interrupts, "We know. You didn't go to that school. But we don't know why that works." They acknowledge that their procedure is rote and laugh in embarrassment, but with good nature.

"Well, let's look at a more familiar one and see if we can figure out why that procedure works." Cathy suggests they look at $\frac{25}{100} = \frac{1}{x}$.

There is brief puzzlement, but then Joanne says, "Oh, of course. It's all about relationships. Whatever you do to twenty-five to get to a hundred, you have to do the same thing to one. That's why you have to divide the twenty-five into one hundred."

Lucienne still looks puzzled. "I still don't get it," she admits.

Ina offers support. "I think it's like—twenty-five is to one hundred like one is to—something else. And we're trying to find the something else."

"But what is the *x* for? I don't get how we moved all these symbols around." Like many teachers, Lucienne's understanding falls apart the minute variables appear, since algebra has primarily been taught only as rote manipulation—rules and procedures—devoid of meaning.

Ina offers an explanation that seems to help. "The *x* is just what we are multiplying twenty-five by. You don't have to move the twenty-five over. You could also say, twenty-five times what will equal one hundred."

Lucienne seems satisfied, so Cathy brings them back to the decimal case in point. "So now let's go back to .142857. What should we do here, Lucienne?"

Lucienne is a bit tentative in her response, but she works it out as she talks about it. "I think we have to find out how many times .142857 goes into—no—how many times 142,857 goes into—one million—is that right? Yes—six zeroes." She counts the places in the decimal with her finger to determine the number of zeroes as she talks.

"Do you all agree?" Cathy looks around at each member of the group. They each nod in agreement, so Lucienne punches the numbers into the calculator.

"It's 7.000007. That's weird. What does that mean—one over 7.000007?" Lucienne is again puzzled, as are the other members of the group. "Oh, wait a minute—I think I'm seeing something here." Lucienne begins to get excited. "Look—the seven repeats after the sixth place! The

$$\frac{142857}{1,000,000} = \frac{1}{x}$$

$$142857x = 1,000,000$$

$$x = \frac{1,000,000}{142857}$$

$$x = 7.000007$$

FIGURE 9.2

decimal repeats, too, after six places! And if you take that seven left and divide it into one—" on the calculator she punches in one divided by seven and produces the repeating decimal. "Yes! Wow, this is cool. Look—the fraction is one seventh. Or the percent could be 14.2857 and one seventh! It will just keep repeating."

Joanne is also intrigued. "I need to check this out with long division. I believe you and I see it with the calculator, but I need to see how and why the pattern repeats." Joanne grabs a pencil, and Cathy leaves them as they set to work. She wanders to the group Willem is with; they are talking about thirds.

Stephanie, a middle school teacher, is explaining how she and the other members of her group know that if $\frac{1}{3}$ is equivalent to .33$\frac{1}{3}$, and .3333 . . . then $\frac{1}{6}$ is equivalent to .16$\frac{2}{3}$ and .16666 . . . They are using a halving strategy just as Pierre, Lena, Barbara, and Kate did earlier.

"And so what about two thirds?" asks Willem.

"It's just double," Stephanie exclaims with confidence. "It's .6666. . . . It keeps repeating, just like the threes in .3333. . . ."

Willem goes on, "So what about .9999 . . . —what is that equal to?"

At first Stephanie is undaunted. "That's three times the one third."

"So that's three thirds?"

"Yes—no—yes—but it can't be. That's one." Stephanie is very perplexed. Willem has succeeded in triggering disequilibrium. "But .9999 . . . is less than one."

Disequilibrium is one of the mechanisms that spurs genuine learning (Piaget 1977). It is, in fact, puzzlement and surprise at results that drive many mathematicians to work on the same problem for years—sometimes a lifetime—exploring relations and constructing proofs. Several mathematicians have even written about this fact. For example, E. C. Titchmarsh once remarked, "Perhaps the most surprising thing about mathematics is that it is so surprising. The rules which we make up at the beginning seem ordinary and inevitable, but it is impossible to foresee their consequences" (cited in Rose 1988). And Godfrey Hardy (1948), in *A Mathematician's Apology*, wrote, "In great mathematics there is a very high degree of unexpectedness, combined with inevitability and economy."

How often have we engaged learners in genuine intrigue and puzzlement, helped them meet the unexpected? In most traditional mathematics classrooms the only puzzlement that occurs is when learners are unclear about what a teacher is explaining. Have we been giving learners opportunities in our classrooms to actually do mathematics—to be young mathematicians at work? Or have we only been teaching the history of mathematics? When teachers have the opportunity to experience genuine mathematical puzzlement and see how it can become the driving force in learning, they are much better able to facilitate it in their classrooms. They learn to enjoy it and to enable their students to enjoy it. As Einstein wrote in an essay entitled "What I Believe," "The most beautiful thing we can experience is the mysterious. It is the source of all true art and science." What initially seemed obvious to Stephanie as she multiplied has now resulted in a mysterious outcome that will become an inquiry for the whole class, one of the big ideas about rational numbers that Willem and Cathy intend to focus on.

Formulating a Vision

Algebra and numerical symbols came about because mathematicians needed to communicate their ideas to one another—to communicate the relationships they noticed. Algebraic symbols can be used in many ways, and mathematicians decide for themselves what relationships to express and how to express them. For teachers to appreciate the feeling of empowerment that comes from building an idea for oneself and to be able to generate this same feeling in their students, they must experience the process. They must learn what it means to work at the edge of their knowledge, to challenge themselves mathematically, to think hard. They must learn that puzzlement is an important process in learning. Teachers must be willing to see themselves as mathematicians and to understand that mathematics is a creative process—one that often demands a struggle. Only then will they really understand the exhilaration and empowerment that comes from doing mathematics—from constructing and mathematizing their world.

Because teachers usually believe that teaching means explaining clearly or that learners will learn if they listen and try to understand what is being explained, they often think a "math congress" is nothing more than a whole-class "share"—a time when learners try to explain their thinking to one another. Although this is partially true—learners do try to explain their thinking—the purpose of the discussion is to continue to deepen everyone's mathematical understanding, particularly those who are sharing, not for some to tell so others will "get it." If learning involves constructing and making sense of ideas for oneself, then telling has little effect, even when one learner is telling another. The teacher must think through the purpose of the congress and orchestrate the sharing accordingly.

Even though these teachers have experienced the joy of constructing ideas for themselves in group work, they still need to experience the process of discussing critical mathematical ideas, exploring similarities between solutions, and modeling situations in alternative ways. With this in mind, Cathy and Willem convene a math congress and ask Stephanie's group to present their strategy and resulting dilemma.

The group members hang their fractions, percents, and decimal equivalents on the line, placing the .9999 . . . just before the numeral 1.

"We know .9999 . . . can't be one. We are sure it is just before it, so we are putting it here," Stephanie begins. "But we also know it is three times one third, and that is one. We are sure of that, too! So now we are not sure of anything!" She laughs as she explains her group's dilemma. Now the whole class is perplexed, and a spirited discussion begins.

"I agree with you that .9999 . . . is before one, so now I am thinking that maybe .3333 . . . is just before one third—and .6666 . . . is just before two thirds," Pierre offers tentatively. Several participants nod in agreement.

"But I am sure that .333 . . . *is* one third," Lucienne states adamantly. "Because when you divide one by three you get the repeating decimal. We did it with one seventh and we got a repeating decimal there, too."

"So you are sure that the quantity of .333 . . . is a rational number equivalent to one third?" Willem writes $.3\overline{3} = \frac{1}{3}$ and $.\overline{142857} = \frac{1}{7}$, introducing the mathematical notation of placing a line over the repeating part of the decimal and the term *rational number*.

Joanne agrees. "Can I come to the board and show what I did?" Without waiting for a response from Willem, she goes to the chalkboard and demonstrates the long division of one divided by three (see Figure 9.3). "You keep getting the digit one left. So it is thirty-three and a third percent, or .3333 . . ." After a moment of quiet she adds almost as an afterthought, "Why did you call $.3\overline{3}$ a rational number?"

Willem provides a definition. "A rational number is a number that can be represented as a fraction, a ratio. For example, one submarine sandwich for three people is one third for each. And you seem to be telling me that this one third is equivalent to thirty-three and a third percent of the sub, or $.3\overline{3}$."

Jules Henri Poincaré once wrote, "Mathematicians do not study objects, but relations between objects. Thus, they are free to replace some objects by others so long as the relations remain unchanged. Content to them is irrel-

FIGURE 9.3
Joanne's Long Division

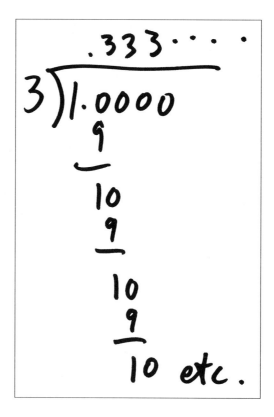

evant: they are interested in form only. . . . Mathematics is the art of giving the same name to different things." Willem is engaging the participants in this art—in grappling with the heart of equivalence, in the relationships between the fraction, percent, and decimal forms of the same quantities.

Jadine is not ready to agree so quickly. "But there is no way that I am willing to accept that .9$\overline{9}$ is equivalent to one!" Jadine is as adamant as Lucienne and Joanne. "It might be just a hairline away, but it is not one! Give me a whole sub, not .9$\overline{9}$!"

"How big is the hairline?" Willem asks with a smile.

"A sliver—the difference—I just know it can't be one!" Jadine replies jokingly.

The renowned mathematician David Hilbert once said, "The infinite! No other question has ever moved so profoundly the spirit of man" (quoted in Newman 1956). To truly understand rational numbers, Kate, Jadine, and the other participants must grapple with the infinite.

Kate, who has been perplexed and quiet thus far, enters the discussion. "To get the difference, Jadine, I think you are stopping the number somewhere." Jadine ponders Kate's thought. Kate continues, "You can't stop the number, or you change it. The minute you make a sliver of a difference, you have stopped the repeating. Like even if the repeating of .9999 et cetera goes to a billion digits. That is a different number than .9$\overline{9}$, which repeats to infinity. I've been sitting here playing with arrays. I made a ten-by-ten array to give myself one hundred squares—just so I could see the percent equivalents. One third is definitely thirty-three and a third percent. See, you get thirty-three squares with one third of the last square." Kate holds up the array shown in Figure 9.4. "So two thirds has to be sixty-six and two thirds percent. So three thirds, the whole thing, is ninety-nine and three thirds percent."

"Oh, my head hurts!" Pierre exclaims. "This is amazing. My whole sense of number and number lines just exploded! What are numbers? Smudges? Does .9$\overline{9}$ smudge into three thirds?"

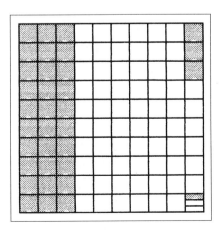

FIGURE 9.4
*Kate's Array Showing
33^1/$_3$% Shaded*

Jadine shakes her head in amazement as well, but she is still somewhat perplexed. "I get the multiplication part, how two thirds is twice $.3\overline{3}$—and your logic—I can even see what ten times that would be—but it is really hard for me to accept that $.9\overline{9}$ is equivalent to one."

Since Jadine has mentioned multiplication by ten, Cathy sees an opportunity to explore with the class the well-known mathematical proof for the equivalence of $.9\overline{9}$ to one. "What *would* ten times $.9\overline{9}$ be?" she asks Jadine.

"Just move the decimal," Jadine responds confidently, "$9.9\overline{9}$."

"So I'll write that down. And let's just call the number x." Cathy writes the equations shown in Figure 9.5 and then guides the group through the proof. "What if we take the difference between these? What will we get?"

"Oh, my god, that's beautiful!" exclaims Pierre, pure amazement on his face. "Nine times the number x equals nine! So x equals one! That means you can substitute one for x and that equals point nine nine bar! What is also amazing to me is that I have a foggy remembrance of having seen that proof before, in a past algebra class somewhere. But I never appreciated it, and I probably also never really understood it. It was something magical that the teacher did with symbols. To some extent it still seems magical—magical manipulation of symbols to prove something. But what I feel so exhilarated about is how my whole sense of number has just changed. And how empowered I feel having worked through this puzzle myself. I feel I own for myself this new sense and appreciation for number. If only I could turn my classroom into such a place of inquiry."

"Thought is only a flash between two long nights, but this flash is everything," Poincaré (cited in Newman 1956) once wrote about mathematical insight. Loving mathematics comes from appreciating puzzlement and seeing the elegance in beautiful proofs. The participants in this institute have been engaging with some hard mathematical ideas—ideas that require grappling with infinity. Their mathematical understanding is being deepened, but they are also beginning to think deeply about their beliefs about teaching and learning. They are beginning to formulate new visions of practice.

FIGURE 9.5

$$10x = 9.\overline{99}$$
$$- \qquad x = .\overline{99}$$
$$\overline{\qquad\qquad\qquad}$$
$$9x = 9$$

Living in a Mathematical World

Being a mathematician means thinking about mathematics outside the classroom as well as in it. It means being willing to work on problems at home, to wonder about them during your commute to work, to raise your own mathematical inquiries. Toward this end, we ask teachers in our workshops and courses to keep double-entry journals. On one side they are to continue the mathematics they have been doing during the day—reflect on other participants' mathematical ideas, do more work on ideas they did not fully understand, raise other questions and/or mathematical inquiries. (We often form inquiry groups around these mathematical questions and pursue them during the institutes.) The other side of the journal is for recording insights about learning and teaching—what enabled them to learn the things they learned, what strategies they might try in their classrooms to help children learn. These pedagogical insights should be connected to the insights related to their own learning: that's why it's a *double*-entry journal. Our aim is to enable teachers to form new beliefs, a new vision of practice, and then help them transform these beliefs into practical strategies—to ground teacher education in an analysis of the connection between learning and teaching.

After the class we've discussed in this chapter, Pierre writes in the mathematics side of his journal:

> I was amazed in class today. My whole sense of numbers, as quantities that I could count, came tumbling down today. Mathematics, art, and philosophy all seem the same! I began thinking about how if all decimals that repeat could be represented as $\frac{1}{x}$, a rational number, then what about numbers that don't repeat? Where do they go on the number line? Can they go on it? Approximations can but then we are stopping the number. It's like transcendentalism, going beyond the real world! I had always told my kids that pi was equal to $\frac{22}{7}$. That can't be right because that would be $3\frac{1}{7}$. And now I know that $\frac{1}{7}$ is equivalent to $.\overline{142857}$; $\frac{1}{7}$ is a rational number. So $\frac{22}{7}$ is rational. But I know pi is irrational because as far as mathematicians have gone, even with computer technology, there is no repeating pattern. Have I been teaching my kids that pi was rational by telling them that it could be represented as $\frac{22}{7}$? And where does pi go on the number line? My head hurts. I haven't done this much thinking about mathematics in years—no—ever. Now I'm thinking that numbers are smudges and philosophical ideas that hold up only if they can be proven. And what about a case of one divided by infinity, does it smudge into zero?

On the pedagogy side of his journal, Pierre reflects on how his own learning will affect his teaching:

> Math was never like this for me. I remember hating it. There was only one way to get an answer and it was the teacher's way. That's

why I majored in English literature. Actually, I had seen that proof before that Cathy guided us through at the end, but when I encountered it long ago it was boring and meaningless. I obviously never understood it, or its importance, or I would have had a better sense of rational numbers and what they were. What a joy it was today to work as a community. Even arguing with each other was fun as we struggled to make sense of things. I hope I can give my kids the same kind of experience. I feel exhilarated and empowered to figure out things for myself. Math now seems creative. Today we imagined in math; we explored relations; we tried to understand and prove our ideas to each other. I don't want my kids to see math as I did, to hate it and think only the answer matters. Today I feel like a mathematician and I want my kids to have that same feeling. I want them to debate, think, inquire, and prove. I want them to see math as creative, as philosophy, as art!

Pierre is beginning to see himself as a mathematician. He is willing to raise and pursue mathematical inquiries—to see the world through a mathematical lens. He is enjoying and appreciating the puzzlement that accompanies genuine learning.

The mathematician Alfréd Rényi once commented, "If I feel unhappy, I do mathematics to become happy. If I am happy, I do mathematics to keep happy" (cited in Turán 1970). And another mathematician, Paul Halmos (1985), noted a similar emotion: "The joy of suddenly learning a former secret and the joy of suddenly discovering a hitherto unknown truth are the same to me—both have the flash of enlightenment, the almost incredibly enhanced vision, and the ecstasy and euphoria of released tension."

In contrast, look again at the Malcolm X quotation used as one of the epigraphs to this chapter: "I'm sorry to say that the subject I most disliked was mathematics. I have thought about it. I think the reason was that mathematics leaves no room for argument. If you made a mistake, that was all there was to it." So many teachers are products of classrooms where no arguments occurred, where mathematics was seen as getting problems correct, as a discipline where the performance of procedures without mistakes was the goal.

Perhaps it is too much to expect to turn every teacher into someone who derives as much joy in doing mathematics as Rényi did. But math anxiety can be lessened when teachers are able to appreciate and take pleasure in creating, in figuring out. As the mathematician J. W. A. Young points out, "Mathematics has beauties of its own—a symmetry and proportion in its results, a lack of superfluity, an exact adaptation of means to ends, which is exceedingly remarkable and to be found only in the works of the greatest beauty. When this subject is properly . . . presented, the mental emotion should be that of enjoyment of beauty, not that of repulsion from the ugly and the unpleasant" (cited in Eves 1988).

For teachers to be able to teach in the ways illustrated in these chapters, they need to walk the edge between the structure of mathematics and child development, between the community and the individual. They need to be willing to live on the edge. There is no one path, no one line, no one map for the journey. The landscape of learning has many paths, and the horizons shift as we approach them. Knowing the landscape, having a sense of the landmarks—the big ideas, the strategies, and the models—helps us plan the journey. We need to structure the environment to bring children closer to the landmarks, to the horizon—to enable them to act on their world mathematically.

Just as mathematics learning needs to be situated in context, in the environment of the landscape, teacher education needs to be situated in the context of teaching/learning. New belief systems and a new vision of practice need to be constructed through subsequent reflection on learning and teaching. Teachers need to see themselves as mathematicians. If we foster environments in which teachers can begin to see mathematics as mathematizing—as constructing mathematical meaning in their lived world—they will be better able to facilitate the journey for the young mathematicians with whom they work.

REFERENCES

Anglin, W. S. 1982. "Mathematics and History." *Mathematical Intelligencer* 4(4).

Beishuizen, M., K. P. E. Gravemeijer, and E. C. D. M. van Lieshout. 1997. *The Role of Contexts and Models in the Development of Mathematical Strategies and Procedures*. Utrecht, the Netherlands: Utrecht University (CD-ß Series on Research in Education; 26).

Bloom, B. S. 1980. *All Our Children Learning*. New York: McGraw-Hill.

Bloom, B. S., and A. W. Foskay. 1967. "Formulation of Hypotheses." In *International Study of Achievement in Mathematics. A Comparison in Twelve Countries,* edited by T. Huson, vol. 1, 64–76. Stockholm: Almqvist and Wiskell.

Bloom, B. S., J. T. Hastings, and G. F. Madaus. 1971. *Handbook on Formative and Summative Evaluation of Student Learning*. New York: McGraw-Hill.

Bodin, A. 1993. "What Does 'to Assess' Mean? The Case of Assessing Mathematical Knowledge." In *Investigations into Assessment in Mathematics Education,* edited by M. Niss, 113–41. Dordrecht, the Netherlands: Kluwer.

Boyer, Carl B. 1991. *A History of Mathematics*. New York: Wiley.

Cobb, P. 1996. "The Mind or the Culture? A Coordination of Sociocultural and Cognitive Constructivism." In *Constructivism: Theory, Perspectives, and Practice,* edited by C. T. Fosnot, ch. 3. New York: Teachers College Press.

———. 1997. "Instructional Design and Reform: A Plea for Developmental Research in Context." In *The Role of Contexts and Models in the Development of Mathematical Strategies and Procedures,* edited by M. Beishuizen, K. P. E. Gravemeijer, and E. C. D. M. van Lieshout, 273–89. Utrecht, the Netherlands: Utrecht University (CD-ß Series on Research in Education; 26).

Davis, P., and R. Hersh. 1981. *The Mathematical Experience*. Boston: Birkhäuser.

DEHN, M. 1983. "The Mentality of the Mathematician: A Characterization." Translated by A. Shenitzer. *The Mathematical Intelligencer* 5(2): 18–26.

DE LANGE, J. 1992. "Critical Factors for Real Changes in Mathematics Learning." In *Assessment and Learning of Mathematics,* edited by G. C. Leder, 305–29. Hawthorn, Victoria: Australian Council for Educational Research.

DESCARTES, R. 1637. *Discours de la méthode pour bien conduire sa raison et chercher la varité dans les sciences plus la diotrique, les meteores, et la geometrie, qui sont des essais de cette methode.* Leyde: I. Maire.

DOLK, M. 1997. *Onmiddellijk onderwijsgedrag over denken en handelen van leraren in onmiddellijke onderwijssituaties.* Utrecht, the Netherlands: W.C.C.

DOWKER, A. 1992. "Computational Estimation Strategies of Professional Mathematicians." *Journal for Research in Mathematics Education* 23(1): 45–55.

DUCKWORTH, E. 1987. *The Having of Wonderful Ideas and Other Essays on Teaching and Learning.* New York: Teachers College Press.

EINSTEIN, ALBERT. Cited in H. Eves 1988. *Return to Mathematical Circles.* Boston: Prindle, Weber and Schmidt.

ENCYCLOPAEDIA BRITANNICA EDUCATIONAL CORPORATION. 1997. *Mathematics in Context. A Connected Curriculum for Grades 5–8.* Chicago: Encyclopaedia Britannica Educational Corporation.

EVES, H. 1988. *Return to Mathematical Circles.* Boston: Prindle, Weber and Schmidt.

FOSNOT, C. T. 1989. *Enquiring Teachers, Enquiring Learners.* New York: Teachers College Press.

———. 1993. "Learning to Teach, Teaching to Learn: The Center for Constructivist Teaching/Teacher Preparation Project." *Teaching Education* 5(2): 69–78.

———, ed. 1996. *Constructivism: Theory, Perspectives, and Practice.* New York: Teachers College Press.

FOSNOT, C. T., AND M. DOLK. 2001a. *Young Mathematicians at Work: Constructing Number Sense, Addition, and Subtraction.* Portsmouth, NH: Heinemann.

———. 2001b. *Young Mathematicians at Work: Constructing Multiplication and Division.* Portsmouth, NH: Heinemann.

FOSNOT, C. T., M. DOLK, AND M. VAN DEN HEUVEL. 2001. "Evaluation of the Mathematics in the City Project: Standardized Achievement Test Results." Paper presented at the annual conference of the American Educational Research Association, Seattle, April.

FREUDENTHAL, H. 1968. "Why to Teach Mathematics So As to Be Useful." *Educational Studies in Mathematics* 1: 3–8.

———. 1973. *Mathematics As an Educational Task.* Dordrecht, the Netherlands: Reidel.

————. 1991. *Revisiting Mathematics Education: The China Lectures.* Dordrecht, the Netherlands: Kluwer.

GAGNÉ, R. 1965. *The Conditions of Learning.* London: Holt, Rinehart, and Winston.

GAUSS, K. F. (1777–1855). 1808. Letter to Bolyai.

GRAVEMEIJER, K. P. E. 1999. "How Emergent Models May Foster the Constitution of Formal Mathematics." *Mathematical Thinking and Learning* 1(2): 155–77.

————. 2000. "A Local Instruction Theory on Measuring and Flexible Arithmetic." Paper presented at the International Conference of Mathematics Educators, Tokyo, Japan; August.

GUEDJ, D. 1996. *Numbers: The Universal Language.* Paris: Gallimard. English translation. 1997. New York: Harry Abrams.

HALMOS, PAUL R. 1985. *I Want to Be a Mathematician.* New York: Springer.

HARDY, GODFREY HAROLD. 1948. *A Mathematician's Apology.* Cambridge: University Press.

HEROCLITUS. Cited in Boyer, Carl B. 1991. *A History of Mathematics.* New York: Wiley.

HERSH, R. 1997. *What Is Mathematics, Really?* London: Oxford University Press.

HILBERT, D. 1897. *Report on Number Theory (Zalbericht).*

————. 1962. *Grundlagen der Geometrie.* Stuttgart: Teubner.

JEANS, SIR JAMES. Quoted in Newman, J. R., ed. 1956. *The World of Mathematics.* New York: Simon and Schuster.

KAMII, C., AND A. DOMINICK. 1998. "The Harmful Effects of Algorithms in Grades 1–4." In *The Teaching and Learning of Algorithms in School Mathematics,* edited by L. Morrow and M. Kenney. Reston, VA: National Council of Teachers of Mathematics.

KANT, E. Cited in D. Hilbert, D. 1962. *Grundlagen der Geometrie.* Stuttgart: Teubner.

KARLIN, S. 1983. Eleventh R. A. Fisher Memorial Lecture. Royal Society, 20 April.

KASNER, E., AND J. NEWMAN. 1940. *Mathematics and the Imagination.* New York: Simon and Schuster.

KORTHAGEN, F., AND J. KESSEL. 1999. "Linking Theory and Practice: Changing the Pedagogy of Teacher Education." *Educational Researcher* 28(4): 4–17.

LEIBNIZ, G. W. (1646–1716). Quoted in Simmons, G. 1992. *Calculus Gems.* New York: McGraw Hill.

LORENZ, J. H. 1997. "Is Mental Calculation Just Strolling Around in an Imaginary Number Space?" In *The Role of Contexts and Models in the Development of Mathematical Strategies and Procedures,* edited by M. Beishuizen, K. P. E. Gravemeijer, and E. C. D. M. van Lieshout, 199–213. Utrecht, the Netherlands: Utrecht University (CD-ß Series on Research in Education; 26).

MA, L. 1999. *Knowing and Teaching Elementary Mathematics.* Mahwah, NJ: Erlbaum.

MITTAG-LEFFLER, G. Quoted in Rose, N. 1988. *Mathematical Maxims and Minims.* Raleigh, NC: Rome.

NATIONAL COUNCIL FOR TEACHERS OF MATHEMATICS. 1989. *Curriculum and Evaluation Standards for School Mathematics.* Reston, VA: NCTM.

———. 2000. *Principles and Standards for School Mathematics.* Reston, VA: NCTM.

NEWMAN, J. R., ed. 1956. *The World of Mathematics.* New York: Simon and Schuster.

PASCAL, B. 1670. *Pensées de Pascal sur la religion et sur quelques autres subjets.* Paris: Garnier. Reprint, Saint Étienne: Éditions de l'Univ. de Saint-Étienne, 1971.

PIAGET, J. 1977. *The Development of Thought: Equilibration of Cognitive Structures.* New York: Viking.

PLATO (ca. 429–347 B.C.). Quoted in Newman, J. R., ed. 1956. *The World of Mathematics.* New York: Simon and Schuster.

POISSON, S. Quoted in *Mathematics Magazine* 64(1), 1991.

POLYÁ, G. (1887–1985). Quoted in *The American Mathematical Monthly* 100(3): 286, 1993.

ROSE, N. 1988. *Mathematical Maxims and Minims,* Raleigh, NC: Rome.

SCHIFTER, D., AND C. T. FOSNOT. 1993. *Reconstructing Mathematics Education: Stories of Teachers Meeting the Challenge of Reform.* New York: Teachers College Press.

SIMMONS, G. 1992. *Calculus Gems.* New York: McGraw Hill Inc.

SIMON, M. 1995. "Reconstructing Mathematics Pedagogy from a Constructivist Perspective." *Journal for Research in Mathematics Education* 26: 114–45.

STREEFLAND, L. 1981. "Cito's kommagetallen leerdoelgericht getoestst" ["Cito's Decimals Tested in a Criterion-Referenced Way"]. *Willem Bartjens* 1(1): 34–44.

———. 1985. "Mathematics As an Activity and Reality As a Source." *Niewe Wiskrant* 5(1): 60–67.

TERC. 1998. *Investigations in Number, Data, and Space.* Palo Alto: Dale Seymour.

TREFFERS, A. 1987. *Three Dimensions: A Model of Goal and Theory Description in Mathematics Instruction.* The Wiskobas Project. Dordrecht, the Netherlands: Reidel.

RÉNYI, ALFRÉD. Cited in P. Turán, "The Work of Alfréd Rényi." *Matematikai Lapok* 21: 199–210, 1970.

VAN DEN HEUVEL-PANHUIZEN, M. 1996. *Assessment and Realistic Mathematic Education.* Series on Research in Education, no. 19 (CD-ROM). Utrecht, the Netherlands: Utrecht University.

VAN DEN HEUVEL-PANHUIZEN, M., AND C. T. FOSNOT 2001. "Assessment of Mathematics Education: Not Only the Answers Count." In *Proceedings of the 25th Conference of the International Group for the Psychology of Mathematics Education*, edited by M. van den Heuvel-Panhuizen, vol. IV, 335–42. Utrecht: Freudenthal Institute.

VAN DEN HEUVEL-PANHUIZEN, M., C. T. FOSNOT, AND M. DOLK 1999. Internal Document, Mathematics in the City Assessment Document. [CE this is an evaluation instrument]

VERSCHAFFEL, L., B. GREER, AND E. DE CORTE. 2000. *Making Sense of Word Problems.* Lisse: Swetz and Zeitlinger.

WILDER, R. L. Cited in The American Mathematical Monthly, v. 101 (1994), no. 3 pg 282.

WOODARD, M. 2000. Mathematical Quotation Server: http://math.furman.edu/~mwoodard/mqs/mquot.shtml.

YACKEL, E. 2001. "Explanation, Justification and Argumentation in Mathematics Classrooms." In *Proceedings of the 25th Conference of the International Group for the Psychology of Mathematics Education*, edited by M. van den Heuvel-Panhuizen, vol. I, 9–24. Utrecht: Freudenthal Institute.

YOUNG, J. W. A. Cited in Eves, H. 1988. *Return to Mathematical Circles,* Boston: Prindle, Weber and Schmidt.

INDEX